GENE TECHNOLOGY

GENE TECHNOLOGY

CONFRONTING THE ISSUES
BY CHRISTOPHER LAMPTON

Series Consultant:
Charles R. Barman

FRANKLIN WATTS
A Science/Technology/Society Book
New York London Toronto Sydney 1990

On the cover: Computer graphics image of deoxyribonucleic acid (DNA), showing its double helix structure and associated water molecules (green). DNA consists of two linked strands of nucleotides (dark blue and purple), coiled into a helix. The strands are joined by the hydrogen bonding of pairs of organic bases (light blue and yellow) on adjacent nucleotides. The organic bases are thymine, adenine, cytosine, and guanine. (Courtesy of Photo Researchers Oxford Molecular Biophysics Laboratory/Science Photo Library.)

Photographs courtesy of: Photo Researchers: pp. 26, 45 (Don Fawcett); Stanford University Visual Art Service: p. 59 top; University of California, San Francisco: p. 59 bottom (Robert Foothorap); Huntington's Disease Society of America: p. 78; AP/Wide World Photo: p. 91; Cold Spring Harbor Laboratory: p. 94; Center for Disease Control: p. 103.

Library of Congress Cataloging-in-Publication Data

Lampton, Christopher.
    Gene technology : confronting the issues / by Christopher Lampton.
       p.   cm. — (A Science/technology/society book)
    Includes bibliographical references and index.
    Summary: Explains the structure of human genetics and discusses how new advances in gene technology will impact society.
    ISBN 0-531-10951-8
    1. Genetic engineering—Juvenile literature.   2. Genetic engineering—Social aspects—Juvenile literature.   3. Molecular genetics—Juvenile literature. [1. Genetic engineering.]
I. Title. II. Series.
QH442.L353   1990
573.2′1—dc20   90-37572   CIP   AC

CONTENTS

PART THREE: SOCIETY

GENE TECHNOLOGY

CHAPTER 1

SCIENCE, TECHNOLOGY, AND SOCIETY

Science. Technology. Society. More than anything else, it is these three things that set human beings apart from other members of the animal kingdom.

Science is the systematic attempt to understand the world around us, to learn the rules by which the universe, including that tiny piece of it in which we live, functions.

Technology is a bit harder to define. In the broadest sense, it refers to the tools we use to change the world around us. Even the simplest tools used by prehistoric humans would qualify as technology under this definition. More commonly, however, we use the word *technology* to mean the ways in which we translate the discoveries of science into a more practical form. In this sense, technology can be described as "applied science." That is how we will use the word in the rest of this book.

Society is the complex network of interactions between human beings, the set of rules and customs that allow us to live in something resembling harmony and to smooth over the inevitable conflicts between individuals as best we can.

Society is very old. It actually predates human beings and is not an exclusive human province; other animals live in social groupings and interact according to social "rules." But humans, given the twin gifts of intelligence and speech, have created a society that is far more complex and adaptable than any organization of nonhuman animals.

SCIENTIFIC METHOD

Science and technology, on the other hand, are relatively new. The quest to understand our environment in a systematic way is quite old, going back at least to the ancient Greeks. But the organized set of rules known as the *scientific method* has been around for only about four centuries, since the time of Galileo and, somewhat later, Sir Isaac Newton. Some historians credit the "invention" of science to the seventeenth-century English philosopher Francis Bacon, whose book *Novum Organum* (1620) detailed a process of reasoning that he called *induction*.

To reason inductively, you must first gather a large amount of data on a subject, usually by performing experiments or making observations, then study that data until certain general rules emerge. The scientific method dictates that you use those general rules to create a *hypothesis*—a formal explanation of the observed phenomena—and use that hypothesis to make specific predictions about the results of future experiments and observations. If those predictions come true, then the general hypothesis that you have induced is probably correct —or, at least, is a close approximation of the truth, which is almost as good. Once the hypothesis has been used to make a substantial number of correct predictions, it is elevated to the status of theory. A theory can never be absolutely proven—the scientific method deliberately leaves room for doubt to allow for future improvements of theories—but if it makes correct predictions, scientists can have confidence in it and can rely on it to guide future observations and hypotheses.

If the predictions based on the hypothesis do not come true, then something is wrong with the hypothesis and it should be modified or scrapped altogether. A hypothesis that generates incorrect predictions will never become a theory.

This is a slow and tedious method of learning about the universe—how much more exciting it would be, for instance, to invent fabulous myths and legends to explain the phenomena that we observe—but it has the advantage of being self-correcting. Inappropriate hypotheses lead to bad predictions and are eliminated. Good hypotheses lead to good predictions and are preserved.

Sometimes the system fails and an inappropriate theory slips through the cracks, but eventually bad theories tend to be caught. Before the development of the scientific method, bad theories tended to hang around forever. The idea that the earth was at the center of the universe and that all other heavenly bodies, embedded in crystalline spheres, circled it survived for nearly two thousand years before it was finally dismissed by such early scientists as Copernicus and Newton.

SCIENCE AND TECHNOLOGY

What is the relationship between science and technology? If we define technology as applied science, then technology and science obviously go hand in hand, with science producing theories about the universe and technology putting those theories into action.

Technology is the creation of practical applications utilizing the rules that science has discovered. If science is the acquisition of pure knowledge, then technology puts that knowledge to work. Science is theory and technology is practice.

That's not always how it works, however. In the real world, an engineer (a person who creates technology) relies as much on his or her own experience as on scientific theory. If something has worked in the past, then the engineer will tend to do it that way again in the future—even if the rules discovered by science imply that it shouldn't work as well as it does. Given a conflict between experience and theory, an engineer will go with experience, unless there are compelling reasons not to.

Nonetheless, science provides a fertile breeding ground for technological ideas that go beyond the experience of any engineer. In this book, we'll talk about how recent developments in the science of biology have created a new technology that would have seemed fantastic as recently as twenty years ago. It is this ability of science to create the framework for new technologies that gives science its greatest impact on society.

SOCIETY

And what is the relationship between science, technology, and society?

Scientific society is as new as science itself. Although ancient humans surely had ideas about what made the universe tick, these ideas were hardly scientific. They were based on inspired guesswork, which was rarely tested by experimentation—and was often quite untestable. Ideas that are untestable (such as the idea that the sun is drawn through the sky by an invisible god riding a heavenly chariot) can never be proven, but they are also difficult to disprove. It's hard to separate the good ideas from the bad.

In recent centuries, however, scientific reasoning has become the main, though not the only, method by which society gains its knowledge of the universe. No one believes today that the sun is pulled through the sky by a god riding a chariot, though a few untestable ideas (such as astrology) persist.

Unlike technology, science consists entirely of ideas, of theories. How, you might ask, can such intangible things as ideas and theories have an effect on the society in which you live?

Very easily, as it happens. You don't have to know much about the history of science to realize that scientific theories have often had a profound impact on society.

In the seventeenth century, for instance, the Catholic church, then an extremely powerful element of European society, brought the Italian astronomer Galileo to trial for insisting that the earth was not in fact at the center of the universe but was merely another planet orbiting the sun. It was the belief of powerful officials that this idea contradicted long-standing church doctrine. Galileo was forced to publicly recant his theories, though he never abandoned them privately.

In the nineteenth century, Charles Darwin's theory of evolution met with similar opposition from religious fundamentalists in Europe and the United

States, an opposition that persists to this very day, although the modern versions of the theory are widely accepted by scientists. Once again, the scientific theory challenged religious beliefs held by a large segment of society. It is quite possible, however, to reconcile both Darwin's theories and the theories of Galileo with the beliefs of most major religions.

Sometimes scientific theories can directly affect the ways in which people interact with one another, though this usually comes about through a misapplication of the theory. Darwin's theory, for instance, spawned a related sociological theory called Social Darwinism. (Darwin himself had nothing to do with Social Darwinism and was not an advocate of the theory.) According to this theory, human societies interact with one another in much the same way as do animals in a jungle or other environment. That is, they struggle for survival and only the fittest survive. The others die out.

Thus, if the British oppressed and occasionally murdered members of the less developed societies that they had colonized, or if white Americans murdered Native Americans and forced them onto reservations to keep them out of the way, this was justified by the "superiority" of the oppressing society. It was nature's way—after all, Darwin said so. (He didn't say this, but advocates of Social Darwinism hardly seemed to care.)

Fortunately, Social Darwinism has fallen out of favor in this century, although there are probably still a few people who believe in it. Darwin's theory, on the other hand, is stronger than ever.

These are only a few of the ways in which the ideas of science have affected society. Looking back over the list, however, it is hard to escape the conclusion that, as often as not, it is the misapplication of scientific ideas that has the most profound effect on society, or at least the most profound negative effect. The poorer our understanding of what scientists are actually saying, the more dangerous the effect on society.

But there is another way in which science can affect society, a much more direct way, and that is by making new technologies possible. The effect of technology on society is direct and profound. Technology, in turn, has a profound effect on society— and, thus, science can indirectly affect society by directly affecting technology.

THE TECHNOLOGICAL REVOLUTION

How does technology affect society? In this century alone, the great technological leaps in communication and transportation, to cite just two examples, have altered deeply the way in which people interact. As we have gained the ability to travel around the world in a matter of hours and to send messages around the planet (and even to and from other planets) in minutes, we have greatly increased the pace at which society can evolve. Decisions that affect large portions of the human race, and that once would have taken years to make, can now be made in days or even minutes. People can travel miles to utilize services that once would have been available to only a few. Computers in our homes and offices bring us information instantaneously that once would have taken years to collect.

Improvements in medical technology also have

had a direct impact on society. More people live to an advanced age now than in the past, changing the very makeup of society. Diseases such as septicemia (blood poisoning caused by infection) and tuberculosis (a debilitating condition of the lungs) were once major killers; now they are usually mild annoyances. Other diseases that were once relatively uncommon, such as cancer and heart failure, are now the leading causes of death, in part because medical science allows people to live long enough to suffer from these conditions.

The ways in which technology has revolutionized our lives are many and varied—too many and varied to list in this book. For the most part, the technological revolution has been a benevolent one; that is, technology has changed our lives for the better. But there is a dark side to the technological revolution. Just as it can change our lives for the better, it can also change them for the worse.

One example is the way in which technology has altered the environment. Thousands of years ago, the earth was covered by a landscape that had evolved over millions of years. Forests, wetlands, tundra, desert—these and other environments circled the globe.

Then humans created technologies that allowed them to change these environments, or that gave them strong reason to do so. Forests were torn down to make way for towns, wetlands were paved over to build industrial areas, deserts were irrigated to create farms. These devastated environments were complex ecosystems. Countless numbers of species of plants and animals had evolved to live in these environments—and many began to die when the environments were taken away. The unrestrained destruction of environments is even now leading to the extinction of vast numbers of plants and animals.

At the same time, factories and machines were being built that released deadly chemicals into the very air that we breathe, or into the waters that we drink. The earth's atmosphere and oceans are so vast that at first they seemed unaffected by this release of chemicals. But as more and more factories and machines have been built, perceptible changes in the atmosphere and oceans have been detected. Not only are the air and water becoming less healthy to breathe and drink, but in some cases, these changes may even be altering the patterns of the weather, which could have devastating consequences.

When we think of ways in which science has had a negative impact on society, perhaps the science that first springs to mind is nuclear physics, which gave us both nuclear power and nuclear weapons. To date, however, the negative effect of these two technologies on society has been more indirect than direct. Nuclear weapons have been used only twice, at the end of World War II. Although the bombings of Hiroshima and Nagasaki were terrible events, they were actually less devastating in terms of lives and property than the earlier firebombing of the city of Dresden, Germany, which was performed with conventional weapons. And, though the threat of nuclear weapons still hangs over our heads long after the end of the war in which they were invented, the fact remains that they have not been used (except in weapons tests) for nearly half a century. With the changing picture in international politics, there is good reason to hope that they will not be used within the lifetime of those reading this book.

Similarly, while some observers are convinced that nuclear power technologies represent a substantial threat to both human lives and the environment, it is nonetheless true that in the nearly forty years that such technologies have been in use, they have killed far fewer people (through radiation poisoning, radiation-induced diseases, etc.) than are killed in automobile accidents every year. (In fact, it can be argued that the automobile is the most devastating of all modern technologies, killing 50,000 people annually in the United States alone. And that figure doesn't include deaths due to automobile-related pollution.)

Thus, while nuclear physics looms large in the public mind as a science that has spawned technologies with a negative impact on society, that impact has been far more psychological than real—so far, anyway. Nonetheless, the potential for abuse exists.

Technology makes our lives better. It improves the quality of our lives, raises our standard of living. No one wants to go back to a time when our ancestors lived in trees or caves or even in log cabins. But, as we have seen, the uncontrolled growth of technology can also make our lives worse and may have long-range negative consequences that no one has yet even imagined.

Society in general has become aware of these consequences only in the latter half of the twentieth century. Until that time, unrestrained technological growth was the rule, not the exception. No one stopped to think about what negative effects a technology might have until that technology was already in place—and was already causing the negative effects.

Now people are realizing that the time to consider the negative effects of technology is before the technology is put to use. We must do our best to predict the impact of new technology in advance and debate what should best be done about it.

Does this mean that we must put our collective feet down and halt the progression of any technology that may have undesirable consequences? No, because nearly all technologies have undesirable consequences, though some have more undesirable consequences than others. And, if we put a stop to all advances in technology, we would be denying ourselves the benefits of those technologies. As we will see later in this book, some of the benefits from future technologies may be considerable.

Rather, we must try to minimize the negative effects and maximize the positive benefits of technology. Most negative consequences come not from the use but the abuse of technology, the unrestrained and irresponsible adoption of advances without consideration of their possible ill effects. If our society is to survive much beyond the twentieth century, we must learn to use technology responsibly, to consider the downside as well as the upside and act accordingly.

In this book, we will look at a new technology that has been spawned by twentieth-century science and that will probably dominate the world of the twenty-first century. It is a technology that will benefit us in amazing ways: by curing diseases now thought incurable, by giving us information about our lives and our health that we would not otherwise have, even by transforming the nature of human beings themselves.

But, like all powerful technologies, this technology has profound possibilities for abuse. It can be used to discriminate against human beings on the basis of their genetic makeup; it can alter and reshape humans and other living organisms in ways both desirable and undesirable; it can create new diseases more devastating than cancer or AIDS. It is, in short, a technology that must be watched carefully, even as it is being developed and put into place.

At the same time, it is a technology that is so important that it should not be dismissed by those who believe it is too dangerous. It is a technology that could put an end to much human suffering and that could make the twenty-first century much more hospitable to human beings.

It is technology of genetics, a technology that deals in the very atoms and molecules of which human beings (and other living organisms) are made. In the next few chapters, we'll look at how scientists and engineers brought this technology into being. Then we'll see some of the ways in which gene technology might be used—and abused—in the decades to come.

Part One
SCIENCE

CHAPTER 2
THE ARITHMETIC
OF LIFE

The word *inheritance* has many meanings. It can refer to the money and possessions that one receives from a parent or other relative when that person dies. It can also refer to less tangible possessions that are passed down from generation to generation, such as a prominent nose or a particular color of hair or even a special attitude toward life.

When we inherit such things from our parents (and their parents and grandparents before them), how are these "possessions" passed down? No one can leave a nose to their child in a will, and there is no way to quantify a special attitude toward life so that it can be divided up among the members of an estate.

In some cases, these things are simply passed along in the environment, so to speak, as one is growing up. You might pick up a special attitude from your parents the same way you pick up any other information—how to tie your shoes, for instance, or how to fasten an earring. Noses and hair color, on the other hand, are passed along in a different manner. They are inherited at birth (or, more properly, at conception), even if they do not become apparent until a somewhat older age. We all know that children tend to resemble their parents. Examine yourself in a mirror and see if you don't look a lot like either your mother or your father—or even both of them.

Another thing that we inherit from our parents, though we tend not to think of it as an inheritance, is our species. Human beings give birth to other human beings, just as cats give birth to cats and fish give birth to fish. If your parents had been cats, then you would be a cat too.

MENDEL AND THE
BIRTH OF THE SCIENCE
OF GENETICS

What is it that we inherit from our parents that determines the shape of our nose, the color of our hair, and our species? As recently as the middle of the last century, no one knew. But in the 1860s, an Augustinian monk named Gregor Mendel suspected that he had the answer—or, at least, the inkling of one.

Mendel, who lived in a monastery in what is now Austria, raised peas in his garden. He studied the way in which certain characteristics, such as red and white flowers or wrinkled and unwrinkled peas, were passed from one generation of plant to the next. What he discovered, using the scientific method of inductive reasoning, was that there were certain rules by which these characteristics were inherited.

For instance, when a pea plant from a long line

of plants with red blossoms was cross-pollinated with a plant with white blossoms, the offspring almost always had red blossoms. But if the offspring were then cross-pollinated with plants with white blossoms, their offspring would sometimes have white blossoms and sometimes red. Furthermore, the ratio of red to white pea plants in this third generation was fairly precise: one white plant to each red plant, when averaged out over a large number of offspring. (Mendel's figures on these ratios were so precise that some modern scientists suspect he exaggerated them a bit.)

Why does it work this way? Mendel guessed that each pea plant must possess some sort of "unit," as he called it, that specified whether its blossoms were red or white. In fact, each must have two such units, one inherited from each parent. If the plant inherited two differing characteristics from each parent—one for red blossoms and one for white— one of the units would override the other. The one that did the overriding Mendel called the *dominant* unit; the one that is overridden Mendel termed the *recessive* unit.

White blossoms were obviously a recessive characteristic; red blossoms were dominant. A plant that possesses both a unit for red blossoms and a unit for white blossoms (one inherited from each parent) will have red blossoms, because the dominant red unit overrides the recessive white unit. A plant with two red units also will have red blossoms. But a plant with two white units will have white blossoms.

Note that only a plant with two white units can have white blossoms, but that a plant with red blossoms may have either two red units or a red and a

white unit. In scientific terminology, we say that a plant with two units for the same characteristic (white blossoms, in this example) is *homozygous* for that characteristic, while a plant with units for two contradictory characteristics (red and white blossoms, in this example) is *heterozygous* for that characteristic. Thus, pea plants with white blossoms are always homozygous for that characteristic, while pea plants with red blossoms may be either homozygous or heterozygous for that characteristic.

Since a pea plant, like many other living organisms, has two parents, it inherits its units from both of them. You'll notice, though, that the two parents have four units between them and that only two are inherited by the offspring. Thus, there must be some sort of selection process that determines which unit the offspring gets from each parent. Since this selection process is random, the offspring has an equal chance of inheriting either characteristic from each parent. If a parent is heterozygous for blossom color —that is, it possesses one unit for red and one for white—the offspring has an equal chance of inheriting either the red or the white unit. If the parent is homozygous for the characteristic, the offspring also has an even chance of receiving either unit—but it hardly matters, since the two units are identical.

What does all this mean? For one thing, it means that when a white plant and a homozygous red plant

Gregor Mendel, an Austrian monk, studied inheritance of traits in pea plants. His work led the way to the modern science of genetics.

are cross-pollinated, the offspring will *always* be a plant with red blossoms, because all of the offspring will be heterozygous for that characteristic (having received a unit for white blossoms from the white parent and a unit for red blossoms from the homozygous red parent). But when a white plant and a heterozygous red plant are cross-pollinated, some of the offspring will be white and some will be red.

Why do these characteristics occur in a fairly precise 50:50 ratio, with half-white and half-red? That's not hard to figure. One of the parents is homozygous for white blossoms, so *all* of the offspring will have at least one white unit. The other parent is heterozygous and thus has a white unit and a red unit. Half of the offspring receive the white (and are therefore homozygous white) and half receive the red (and are therefore heterozygous red). Thus, the ratio is 50:50—when averaged over a large number of offspring, of course.

Mendel observed seven different characteristics of the pea plants and found that they were all inherited according to these ratios. Mendel decided that the plants must have units for all of these characteristics, and also probably for other characteristics that he had not studied.

Mendel wrote up the results of his experiments and published them in an obscure scientific journal, where they were ignored for a third of a century. He mailed a copy to Charles Darwin, who had briefly discussed inheritance in his book *The Origin of Species*, but Darwin never read it. If he had, it may well have speeded up the scientific understanding of inheritance.

Fortunately, Mendel's theories (and his article) were rediscovered in the year 1900, though Mendel had long before passed away. The beginning of the twentieth century thus saw the birth of a new science: *genetics*, the study of physical inheritance. The name of this new science led to a new name for Mendel's *units*: now they were called *genes*.

THOMAS HUNT MORGAN AND MOLECULAR GENETICS

In the 1920s, an American biologist named Thomas Hunt Morgan (1863–1931) studied the way that characteristics were inherited among fruit flies, much as Mendel had studied pea plants. Morgan learned that the genes of fruit flies behaved in the same predictable ways as the genes of pea plants, but he noticed something else as well. Certain genes were inherited together more often than random chance said they ought to be.

According to Mendel, genes were independent. That is, the fact that a pea plant inherited red or white blossoms from a parent had no effect on whether it inherited wrinkled or unwrinkled skin from that same parent. According to Morgan, however, the genes were not entirely independent. Inheriting certain characteristics increased the fruit fly's chance of inheriting other characteristics, if his experiments were to be believed.

As it turned out, Morgan had discovered an important clue to the actual nature of the gene. The study of genetics from Mendel to Hunt is now termed *classical genetics*, a turn of phrase that has a certain nostalgic ring to it. Inadvertently, Morgan had opened the door to a new kind of science: *molecular genetics*.

CHAPTER 3
THE MACHINERY OF LIFE

What are genes? Do they have an actual physical existence, or are they theoretical concepts that scientists can talk about but never touch? Can they be seen, with the naked eye or through a microscope, or are they invisible?

To Mendel, the gene (or unit) was basically a theoretical concept. Though he must have realized that there was an actual, tangible "thing" tucked away somewhere inside his pea plants that represented the physical manifestation of the concept he called a unit, he probably had no idea where that thing was. Perhaps he believed that the actual physical gene would never be found.

GENES AS INFORMATION

In the purest Mendelian sense, the gene is information. We can imagine it as a kind of note that says "This plant will have red blossoms" or "This plant will have white blossoms." But notes must be written in some kind of language and they must be written on some kind of medium. The notes that students pass between themselves in class, for instance, are written in the language that we call English (or French or German or Russian or whatever language the note-passing students speak), and the medium on which the notes are written is usually paper. The notes that you type with a word processor (such as the one being used to type this book) are written in whatever language you speak (probably English, the language in which this book is written) and are written on an electronic medium contained within the circuitry of the computer.

In what language, then, are the "notes" of inheritance written? And on what medium are they written? Happily, this is a question that has been almost entirely answered by twentieth-century biologists.

To answer it, however, it was necessary to look beyond the simple mathematics of Mendelian inheritance and to study the actual material of which living creatures are made. And to understand how that material works, we'll first have to talk about *cells*.

All living things are made of cells, from the smallest single-celled plants and animals (which, as the name implies, are made of only one cell) to the largest land and sea animals (which are composed of trillions of cells). The cell is the smallest thing that deserves to be called "living."

BUILDING BLOCKS
OF CELLS

Like all things on earth, cells are made up of *molecules*, long chains of atoms. (Atoms are the infinitesimally tiny building blocks of matter. They combine in a process called *bonding,* by which a kind of electromagnetic "sticky spot" on the surface of one atom clings to a similar sticky spot on the surface of another.) The difference between the molecules that make up cells and the molecules that make up other things is chiefly one of size. The molecules in a cell are made up of hundreds, thousands, even millions of atoms. In most cases, these immense chains of atoms are twisted back on themselves to form complicated structures with three-dimensional shapes.

The largest units are *polymers,* complex molecules made up of chains of smaller molecules called *monomers.* One of the most important types of polymer is *protein.* Protein molecules are chained together by smaller molecules called *amino acids.* Although there are many different types of amino acids found in nature, only twenty different kinds are used to build proteins. They are listed in Table 1.

The number of different protein molecules that can be formed with these amino acids is staggeringly large. Just as the twenty-six letters of the alphabet can be strung together to form an almost uncountable number of sentences, so the number of possible chains of proteins is almost unimaginably huge (especially when we consider that proteins can contain many thousands of amino acids).

How are these protein molecules used? Some of them are structural, the "beams" and "girders" that keep a cell from collapsing. But most of them are some form of *enzyme,* little molecular machines that perform the work that keeps the cell—and the organism of which it is part—alive.

The main job of enzymes is to promote *chemical reactions,* to help take apart and put together other molecules. The way in which enzymes do this is by

TABLE 1
THE AMINO ACIDS

Alanine	Threonine
Isoleucine	Tryptophan
Hydroxyproline[a]	Valine
Methionine	Histidine
Tyrosine	Arginine
Leucine	Asparagine[b]
Lysine	Serine
Cystine	Glutamine[c]
Cysteine	Proline
Phenylalanine	Glycine

[a] Hydroxyproline is proline with a hydroxy (OH) group.
[b] Activated form: aspartic acid.
[c] Activated form: glutamic acid.

providing a properly shaped surface on which these reactions can take place. (Remember that protein molecules fold back on themselves and therefore have a three-dimensional shape.) Because life itself is essentially a series of chemical reactions, it is the enzymes that make the cells "alive."

In a typical enzymatic reaction, that is, a chemical reaction mediated by an enzyme, the enzyme may lock onto a molecule and hold it in the correct position for it to react with another molecule. Or it may grab hold of both molecules simultaneously, forcing them to come together physically. There are enzymes that break the molecules into smaller molecules, which are then free to come together in new ways. There are other enzymes that carry out a combination of these activities.

There is a second type of polymer that is also important to the cell: *deoxyribonucleic acid*, or DNA for short. Just as protein molecules are chains of amino acids, so DNA molecules are chains of *nucleotides*, which contain a sugar, a phosphate group, and one of four nitrogen bases: adenine, guanine, thymine, and cytosine. These are commonly referred to by their initials A, G, T, and C.

In every cell of every living creature is found a set of DNA molecules, called *chromosomes*. The name means "colored bodies" and comes from the fact that they must be dyed to be seen through a microscope. Chromosomes are found in a special compartment in the middle of the cell called the *nucleus*. As we shall see in a moment, there are other DNA molecules in the cell, but the chromosomes are the most conspicuous and, arguably, the most important.

DNA REPLICATION

One of the most remarkable things that DNA molecules can do is duplicate themselves. Living creatures grow when their cells split apart to form new cells, and each of these new cells needs a complete set of chromosomes. The chromosomes provide this new set by copying themselves. How the chromosomes do this was discovered in 1953, when the American biochemist James Watson and the British scientist Francis Crick unveiled the *double helix* structure of DNA.

A DNA molecule is made up of two strands of

nucleotides, wound about one another in a cork-screwlike manner called a double helix. The nucleotides in one strand of the double helix are bonded to the nucleotides in the opposite strand in much the same manner as the nucleotides in a single strand are bonded to one another. But the shapes of the bases are such that adenine (A) bonds only with thymine (T) and guanine (G) only with cytosine (C). Thymine cannot bond with guanine, adenine cannot bond with cytosine. This is called *base pairing*.

If you were reduced to the size of a molecule and allowed to study the sequence of bases on a strand of DNA, it would seem essentially random. (It isn't really random, as we will see in a moment, but this would not be immediately obvious.) However, whatever sequence is on one strand determines the sequence that is on the other strand, by the rules of base pairing. For instance, if one strand contains the sequence adenine guanine adenine cytosine thymine (AGACT), then the other strand must contain the sequence thymine cytosine thymine guanine adenine (TCTGA). In effect, the strands are complementary images of one another. And, just as a photographic negative can be used to create new copies of a photograph, so can these DNA strands be used to create new copies of a chromosome.

When a cell splits to form new cells, the two strands of the double helix break apart, unzipping from one end of the chromosome to the other. Loose nucleotides floating in the fluid interior of the cell almost immediately bind to the nucleotides in the two strands, forming two more strands, one for each of the complementary images. Because these loose nucleotides bind to the strands according to the rules of base pairing, the two new strands are complementary images of the strands that they bind to. Thus, once the double helix finishes unzipping and the loose nucleotides finish binding to the two original strands, we actually have two new double helixes, identical to the originals. The chromosomes have duplicated themselves.

Of course, mistakes will sometimes happen in this process and the two new helixes may not be perfectly identical. Fortunately, the cell contains a class of enzymes that are capable of "proofreading" the new chromosomes and repairing any errors that they find. The very few mistakes that slip past these proofreaders are called *mutations* and can result in dead cells, certain forms of cancer, even unexpected evolutionary changes. As we will see later, these mistakes can sometimes reside in the cells for many generations, emerging only occasionally to create devastating diseases.

What is it about the chromosomes that makes it so important that they be duplicated so that every cell can have a copy? It's not as though the chromosomes actually *do* anything, in the sense that enzymes do things. They don't rush about the cell, promoting chemical reactions. Rather, the chromosomes are a kind of library. They are the repository of the genes. The genetic information that determines what color our eyes are and what species we belong to is written in the chromosomes, in the very order of the nucleotides themselves.

CHAPTER 4
THE LANGUAGE
OF LIFE

The work of Thomas Hunt Morgan provided valuable clues that the genes were somehow chained together inside the living cell and that the site of those chains was the chromosomes. By the 1940s it had been more or less proven that the medium in which the genes were "written" was DNA.

THE GENETIC CODE

But in what language was this *genetic information* written? How could the fact that a certain organism would have white blossoms or blue eyes or brown skin be encoded in a molecule of DNA?

Before we answer these questions, let's consider how information is encoded in a book such as this one. When you picked up this book, you were probably interested in learning something about gene technology. But what you found when you opened this book was patterns of ink on paper. This probably didn't surprise you, since you've seen similar patterns in other books, but it's fair to ask what such patterns of ink have to do with gene technology—or any other subject, for that matter.

The answer is that the ink itself has nothing to do with gene technology—it's all in the patterns. Indeed, this book could as readily have been written in patterns of rock on sand or clouds against sky, but that would be a lot more expensive (and awkward) to write, not to mention reproduce.

But what is it about the patterns that's so important? If you were to look at a French or German translation of this book, you would see different patterns of ink on the page, but it would still be the same book. If neither the ink nor the specific pattern is important, what's the point in reading a book?

Certain patterns have been agreed upon by certain societies to represent certain information, and thus those patterns can be used to convey information about those things. The society of people who speak English, for instance, has agreed that the particular patterns used in writing this book will represent certain information. Since you are a member of that society and have spent many years learning what these patterns represent, you can read this book and take away information from it.

A set of patterns that can be put together in new and varied ways to convey complex information is called a *language*. The best known languages are the so-called natural languages, which are used by human beings to communicate with one another. English is the natural language spoken (and written) by the author of this book, but there are many other natural languages: French, German, Russian, Chinese, Swahili, Choctaw, and so on. All of these are sets of patterns, both verbal and written, agreed upon by a society to represent certain things, thus, they can be used by members of those societies to communicate among themselves.

There are other kinds of languages. Computer languages, for instance, are patterns agreed upon by designers to represent certain operations that can be performed by computers. Programmers who are familiar with these languages can use them to "tell" a computer what they want it to do. Computer language is not a natural language; it is an artificial one.

The language of the genes is a very natural language, but it was not invented by human beings. Indeed, it predated the existence of humans by hundreds of millions, perhaps even billions, of years. It came about by slow evolution. Once it had evolved, however, it worked so well that nature has left it essentially unchanged since the days when the earth was populated exclusively by single-celled organisms. The cells of all living creatures on earth today use this language and can, in a few circumstances, use it for communicating across vast evolutionary distances. (In the case of viruses, this interspecies communication can have dramatic and often deadly results, as we will see in a moment.)

CRACKING THE GENETIC CODE

The language of the genes is called the *genetic code*. The "books" in which messages are written in this language are the chromosomes themselves.

In simplest terms, a chromosome is a kind of recipe book. It contains a set of directions for making protein molecules. Protein molecules, you will recall, are chains of amino acids. Thus, the recipe for a protein molecule is simply a list of the amino acids that make up that molecule, in the order in which they occur in the chain.

The A, G, C, and T nitrogen bases of nucleotides are the letters of the alphabet in which these recipes are written. The words of the genetic language are called *codons*. Whereas words in the English language can contain varying numbers of letters, from as few as one (in the words *a* and *I*) to a couple of dozen (in words like *antidisestablishmentarianism*), all the words in the genetic language have the same number of "letters": three. This is important, because there are no "spaces" between the words of the genetic language to indicate where one word ends and the next begins. Because all the words are three letters long, no spaces between words are needed.

Each DNA codon represents the name of a single amino acid. Table 2 shows the complete list of three-letter codons and the amino acids that they represent. This chart, which took biologists about ten years to deduce after Watson and Crick discovered the double helix structure of DNA, is one of the greatest achievements of modern science. In effect, it represents the translation of the genetic code into English.

You'll notice that there are many "synonyms" in the chart; that is, several different codons can represent the same amino acid. This is apparently nature's way of guarding against mistakes in the copying of chromosomes, since in many cases an error in copying a codon will produce another codon that means the same thing. (Also, there are sixty-four possible three-letter codons and only twenty amino acids, so there was lots of room for redundancy. There is reason to believe that more primitive versions of the genetic code, which may have existed hundreds of millions of years ago, might have used only two nucleotides per codon, with the third codon being a "space between words" and therefore irrelevant to the meaning of the codon.) You'll also notice that one of the codons simply means "stop." This is the genetic code's equivalent of a period, except that instead of indicating the end of a sentence it indicates the end of a protein recipe.

One recipe for a single protein molecule is now called a gene. This is not quite the same thing that Mendel meant when he referred to a "unit" or that Thomas Hunt Morgan meant when he referred to a "gene," but in many cases the difference is insignificant. A single protein molecule might well make the difference between a pea plant with white blossoms and a pea plant with red blossoms, though other characteristics (such as skin color) might be the results of several genes working in concert. (It is important to note that some genes are also very much influenced by the environment in which they work. A gene in a malnourished organism, for instance, may produce very different results than a gene in a healthy organism.)

A single chromosome is made up of many different genes coding for many different protein molecules. You will recall, however, that Mendel determined that each of us has two genes for each characteristic (which, in this modern sense, means two genes for each protein molecule). Thus, chromosomes are always observed to come in pairs. Human beings have twenty-three pairs of chromosomes, for a total of forty-six chromosomes. Fruit flies have four pairs. Every cell therefore has two

TABLE 2
THE GENETIC CODE

Nucleotides	Amino Acids
UUU	phenylalanine
UUC	phenylalanine
UUA	leucine
UUG	leucine
UCU	serine
UCC	serine
UCA	serine
UCG	serine
UAU	tyrosine
UAC	tyrosine
UAA	stop
UAG	stop
UGU	cysteine
UGC	cysteine
UGA	stop
UGG	tryptophan
CUU	leucine
CUC	leucine
CUA	leucine
CUG	leucine
CCU	proline
CCC	proline
CCA	proline
CCG	proline
CAU	histidine
CAC	histidine
CAA	glutamine
CAG	glutamine
CGU	arginine
CGC	arginine

Nucleotides	Amino Acids
CGA	arginine
CGG	arginine
AUU	isoleucine
AUC	isoleucine
AUA	isoleucine
AUG	methionine
ACU	threonine
ACC	threonine
ACA	threonine
ACG	threonine
AAU	asparagine
AAC	asparagine
AAA	lysine
AAG	lysine
AGU	serine
AGC	serine
AGA	arginine
AGG	arginine
GUU	valine
GUC	valine
GUA	valine
GUG	valine
GCU	alanine
GCC	alanine
GCA	alanine
GCG	alanine
GAU	aspartic acid
GAC	aspartic acid
GAA	glutamic acid
GAG	glutamic acid
GGU	glycine
GGC	glycine
GGA	glycine
GGG	glycine

copies of every recipe. Only in a few cases are these recipes different, in which case the dominant copy takes precedence over the recessive.

PROTEIN SYNTHESIS

For a recipe to be useful, there must be a cook—someone or something to turn the recipe into a meal (or, in this case, a protein molecule). The process of turning a DNA recipe into a protein molecule is called *protein synthesis*. The cook that does the synthesizing is a molecule called a *ribosome*, aided and abetted by several other molecules made out of a substance called *ribonucleic acid*, or RNA for short.

As the name would seem to indicate, RNA is a lot like DNA. Indeed, it is a polymer made of four different kinds of nitrogen bases quite similar to those that make up DNA molecules. The major difference is that RNA uses uracil (U) instead of thymine (T). Like thymine, uracil bonds with adenine and only adenine, according to the rules of base pairing.

There are several different kinds of RNA molecule. The first one involved in the process of protein synthesis is called *messenger RNA* (mRNA). When protein synthesis begins, the section of the chromosome that contains the recipe for that protein is split open by an enzyme and a negative copy of one

Ribosomes (black dotlike structures) in a pancreas cell. Ribosomes synthesize proteins with the help of RNA.

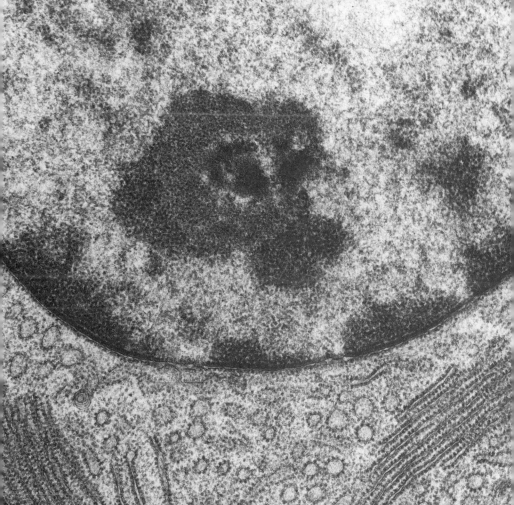

strand of the recipe is made using mRNA nucleotides (rather than DNA nucleotides, as when the chromosomes replicate). You might think of this as the natural equivalent of a photocopying machine, a way of making a quick copy of a valuable original.

Once the copy is complete, it is removed from the DNA, the chromosome is put back together, and the mRNA copy of the gene is released into the body of the cell, where it seeks out (or, more precisely, is found by) a ribosome. A ribosome is a large molecule composed of protein and RNA. It attaches itself to the end of the strand of mRNA, where the first codon in the recipe is located. It then begins to look for an appropriate molecule of *transfer RNA* (tRNA).

The molecules of tRNA are rather unusually shaped, with a sequence of three bases on one end called an *anticodon* and a kind of "hook" codon on the other end designed for snaring a specific type of amino acid. The anticodon consists of the complementary RNA image of one of the codons on a strand of mRNA, and the type of amino acid that the "hook" is designed to snare is the type of amino acid for which that codon stands. For instance, suppose the anticodon contains the sequence of bases AGU. The negative image of that, according to the rules of base pairing, would be UCA, which is the codon that stands for the amino acid serine. Thus, the tRNA molecule with the anticodon AGU would have a hook for snaring serine molecules on the other end.

When the ribosome attaches itself to the mRNA molecule, it "reads" the first codon in the recipe, finds a tRNA molecule with the corresponding anticodon (and the appropriate amino acid hooked to the other end), and attaches it to the mRNA codon. Then it moves forward three nucleotides so that it can read the next codon. It continues this process until it has traveled the full length of the mRNA molecule.

As the ribosome is attaching the tRNA molecules to the mRNA molecule, it is also busily attaching the amino acids at the other end of the tRNA molecules to each other, forming a protein molecule. As the amino acids bind to each other, they break away from the tRNA, forming a free-floating protein molecule, which folds back on itself into a three-dimensional shape.

And that is the process of protein synthesis, the process by which the information in the DNA of the chromosomes is converted into the protein molecules that keep living organisms alive. Because it is these protein molecules that determine whether you have black or blond hair, green or blue eyes, and whether you are a human being or a gerbil, it is the process of protein synthesis that makes you what you are. It is the information in the chromosomes passed to you by your parents at the time of your conception that determines much of what you will be as you grow up.

Of course, there is considerable debate as to just how much of what you are is determined by your chromosomes. As we said earlier, such things as your attitude toward life are determined by the environment in which you grow up (though it is possible that such things can also be influenced to some extent by your chromosomes). However, most of your physical attributes are inherent in your genes, even if they can be influenced to some degree by your environment.

Since we now understand the language that our genes are written in, it would seem an almost trivial thing to read what's written in the genes and learn all of the amazing secrets that go into making a human being. Well, it's not that trivial, but it can be done. Perhaps more amazingly, it is also becoming possible to rewrite the message in the gene, to change the information that makes an organism what it is.

It is these two activities—the reading and re-writing of the genetic information in the cell—that constitute what we call gene technology. And that is the subject of the rest of this book.

Part Two
TECHNOLOGY

CHAPTER 5
ENGINEERING
THE GENE

Up to this point we've talked about the scientific side of genetic research, the acquisition of pure knowledge about the genes. Most of what we've discussed here was known to scientists by the mid-1960s. Although it is fascinating knowledge, answering many questions that had been asked by scientists and philosophers for centuries, this information had relatively little impact on society in general. In fact, the average person on the street would probably be hard put to explain how the genetic code works or how genetic information is transformed into protein molecules, since such knowledge has relatively little impact on the average person's life.

This is not the same as saying that the average person is not affected by the behavior of his or her genes. Obviously the activity of the DNA and protein molecules in an individual's cells is of paramount importance to that individual; he or she would die instantly if that activity were to stop. But genes and enzymes go their merry way whether or not the organism of which they are part has the foggiest notion of how they work.

But new scientific knowledge often leads to new technologies and new technologies can have a very definite impact on the average person's life. Indeed, the new technologies based on our knowledge of the genes may turn out to have an unusually powerful impact on society.

GENETIC INFORMATION VS. GENETIC ENGINEERING TECHNOLOGIES

In this book, we'll talk about two kinds of genetic technology, those based on reading the genes (which we term genetic information technologies) and those based on actually altering the genes (which we term genetic engineering technologies). We'll talk about genetic information technologies in chapters 7 and 8. In this and the next chapter, and in the last chapter of the book, we'll talk about genetic engineering technologies. We'll see some of the ways in which these two technologies may come together to change the face of future medicine.

But first a word about viruses, nature's own genetic engineers.

THE VIRUS HIJACKERS

Viruses are not "alive" by conventional definition, though they have certain things in common with living organisms. They have genes, for instance, held together by a coat of protein. In fact, that is all that a virus is, a protein shell surrounding a tightly coiled strand of DNA (or, in some cases, RNA) that contains the genetic information needed for constructing new copies of the virus. Despite the remarkable simplicity of its design, a virus can do amazing, and sometimes quite terrible, things with this minimal assortment of tools.

Although the viral DNA contains the instructions for building a new virus, the virus itself does not contain the protein-synthesizing equipment needed for making those new copies of itself. It contains no ribosomes, for instance, or mRNA and tRNA molecules. In order to make copies of itself, it must hijack the protein-synthesizing equipment of a living cell and force that cell to make the copies.

On the protein coat of a virus are mounted sharp protrusions that the virus uses for attaching itself to the surface of a cell and injecting its DNA into the cell. (Some viruses amount to little more than natural hypodermic needles for injecting viral DNA into cells.) Once the DNA is inside the cell, the natural protein-synthesizing equipment of the cell will begin blindly making copies of the proteins coded for by the DNA, thus making new copies of the virus itself. The cell will rapidly fill up with these copies of the virus and will ultimately "explode," releasing the copies into the intracellular fluid where they can proceed to infect other cells in the same manner, forcing them to make still more copies of the original virus.

Different types of viruses attach to different types of cells, depending on the shapes of their protein coats and the nature of the sharp protrusions on the outside of the coats. Viruses that attach to human cells are responsible for many of the diseases from which human beings suffer, such as colds and measles. The symptoms of these diseases are caused in part by the destruction wrought by the virus as it takes over cells in order to make copies of itself and in part by the body's own immune system as it fights off the attack.

Certain types of viruses called *retroviruses* mount a somewhat more sophisticated attack on cells. The genes of a retrovirus are stored in RNA rather than DNA. When these genes are injected into a cell, they do not immediately make copies of themselves. Rather, they produce enzymes that copy the viral RNA into DNA strands and splice those strands into the cell's chromosomes, making the viral genes part of the cell's own collection of genes.

Then, whenever the cell divides to produce new cells, it copies the viral genes right along with the cell's own genes, so that each copy of the cell also includes the viral genes. Months or years later, the viral genes will suddenly be activated and will begin producing new copies of the virus. By this time, however, there will be so many copies of the original viral genes spread throughout so many copies of the original cell that the resulting onslaught of viruses can completely overwhelm the immune system of the organism through which the viruses have spread.

Acquired immune deficiency syndrome (AIDS) is believed to be caused by a retrovirus, as is Alzheimer's disease, a degenerative disease of the brain cells that causes memory loss. The AIDS retrovirus is a particularly crafty organism, since the cells that it attacks are part of the body's own immune system; thus, it destroys the very mechanism that would ordinarily be used to rout it from the body.

RESTRICTION ENZYMES: MOLECULAR SCISSORS

Needless to say, our bodies have many weapons with which they can fight attacking viruses. Often, this battle is so swift and successful that we are not even aware that our cells have been the subject of a viral attack. One of the weapons that cells use to fight off viruses is a *restriction enzyme.*

A restriction enzyme is a protein molecule designed to serve as a kind of molecular scissors. Its job is to slice viral DNA (or RNA) into pieces, so that it cannot be used to produce new copies of the virus. It does its job with great precision, seeking out specific sequences of nucleotides in the viral DNA and cutting at specific points in those sequences, rendering the viral DNA harmless.

In the early 1970s it came to the attention of several biologists studying molecular genetics that restriction enzymes could be used as a tool for more than just fighting off viruses. They could be used by scientists to edit and splice existing strands of DNA in very precise ways, much as a film editor edits and splices a motion picture. In effect, restriction enzymes could be used to perform genetic engineering.

One of the first scientists to adopt this technique—possibly the very first—was Paul Berg of Stanford University. In 1971 Berg was studying a virus called SV40 that causes cancer in certain animals (though not in humans). Berg wanted to study the viral genes to learn what sort of proteins they produce, but he wanted to isolate them from the virus itself in order to study them one at a time.

His solution was to use restriction enzymes to slice the desired genes out of the viral DNA, then to use similar enzymes to slice the genes of a *bacterium* (a kind of single-celled organism) and to splice the two sets of genes together. When reinserted into a bacterium the genes would begin producing the viral proteins in such a way that Berg could study them in isolation. In effect, he would be creating a new species of bacteria, a hybrid bacterium that possessed both bacterial genes and viral genes, making it part bacterium and part virus.

He never performed the experiment.

Why not? A graduate student of Berg's, Janet Mertz, attended a workshop on tumor viruses in New York that same year, where she met the microbiologist Robert Pollack, who had a strong interest in the subject of ethics in science. She told Pollack about Berg's experiment. He was furious. Hadn't anyone considered, he asked, the possibility that something might go terribly wrong with such an experiment?

Bacteria commonly infect humans and other living organisms. The bacterium into which Berg intended to splice his hybrid genes was *Escherichia coli* (*E. coli*), which normally lives benignly in human intestines, not causing disease but living symbiotically—cooperatively—with the cells of our bodies. The genes that Berg intended to splice into this bacterium came from a virus that routinely causes cancer in monkeys. What if he accidentally succeeded in creating a bacterium that was capable of causing cancer—in humans?

There was no evidence that the bacterium Berg intended to create would actually be capable of causing cancer. But there was no evidence that it wouldn't, either. What Pollack was saying was that Berg should not plunge blindly into the experiment without first determining what the ramifications might be.

Pollack telephoned Berg and pleaded with him to postpone the experiment. Berg did so reluctantly, but after speaking to a number of his colleagues he realized that the dangers Pollack spoke of were not necessarily as fantastic as he had at first thought. Realizing that other scientists were probably working on similar experiments, Berg turned his thoughts to somehow communicating Pollack's fears to his fellow biologists around the world.

THE BIRTH OF RECOMBINANT DNA TECHNOLOGY

Other scientists were indeed working on similar experiments. Stanley Cohen at Stanford and Herbert Boyer at the University of California at San Francisco had together developed a series of techniques, similar to those Paul Berg had proposed using, that soon came to be called *recombinant DNA*. The secret of recombinant DNA lies in a tiny ring of DNA commonly found in bacterial cells called a *plasmid*.

Usually, the genetic information in a cell is contained within its chromosomes. But bacterial cells often possess additional genes in tiny loops of DNA called plasmids that float around freely through the cell, producing proteins all the while. These plasmids can be passed from one bacterium to another in a process that resembles the way in which higher organisms spread genes among themselves through sexual reproduction. The plasmids themselves can reproduce in much the same manner as chromosomes reproduce, so that a cell may contain several copies of a given plasmid.

Typically, a plasmid will contain genes that are not essential to the survival of the bacterium but that can be extremely useful under certain circumstances. Plasmids containing genes for antibiotic resistance, for instance, have become increasingly common in the years since the invention of penicillin. (Antibiotics are drugs specially intended to kill bacterial cells.)

Bacteria carrying plasmids that confer antibiotic resistance are more likely to survive antibiotic treatment than bacteria that do not. Because of this, such plasmids are more likely to be passed on to other bacteria and thus will become quite common.

Boyer and Cohen realized that plasmids would provide an excellent vehicle for studying genes edited out of other organisms using restriction enzymes. First, they would remove the gene from the original carrier—a virus, another bacteria, or even a human body cell. Then they would splice it into a

Stanley Cohen (above) and Herbert Boyer (below) were pioneers in recombinant DNA technology, the creation of a new DNA molecule by the process of cleaving and rejoining different DNA strands.

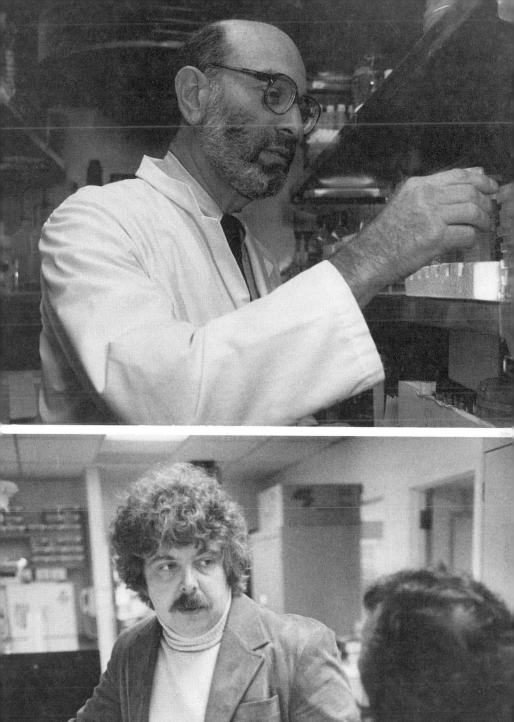

plasmid and inject this *recombinant plasmid* into a bacterial cell, where the gene would begin to express itself, that is, to synthesize the protein for which it coded. The protein could then be studied in isolation.

The two researchers first performed a recombinant DNA experiment in 1973, when they combined a plasmid from a staphylococcus bacterium and a gene from a toad and inserted the result into an *E. coli* bacterium. This experiment represented the beginning of modern genetic engineering.

Then, much to their surprise, Cohen and Boyer, and other scientists working in this area, were asked to halt their experiments at once.

CHAPTER 6
ASSESSING
THE RISKS

In 1973, Paul Berg and Robert Pollack organized a meeting of biologists to be held at the Asilomar Conference Center in Pacific Grove, California. One hundred specialists in tumor research attended and began a tentative discussion of the use of genetic engineering techniques to study cancer genes in living cells.

Was the research dangerous? Nobody was sure. The major result of this Asilomar conference was the scheduling of a second conference, eventually to be called Asilomar II, at which a larger number of biologists would assess the dangers of genetic engineering.

Between these two conferences, the Gordon Research Conference on Nucleic Acids was held and was attended by Herbert Boyer, who was even then pioneering recombinant DNA techniques. It was also attended by Maxine Singer, a friend of Paul Berg's and a research chemist at the National Institutes of Health (NIH).

When Boyer discussed his use of genetic engineering techniques, Singer realized that they were essentially the same as those that Paul Berg had refrained from using. She immediately drafted a statement asking scientists to halt such work until the risks could be assessed, but by the time it was read to the conference many of the biologists had gone home. The remaining biologists voted to send a letter to the journal *Science*, published by the American Association for the Advancement of Science (AAAS), officially urging biologists to declare a moratorium on recombinant DNA research.

The National Academy of Sciences then asked Paul Berg to chair a committee to study recombinant DNA techniques. The committee, made up of several prominent biologists, many of whom were or were later to become Nobel Prize winners, recommended that all recombinant DNA research be suspended until after the second Asilomar conference.

The letter worked. Biologists, in many cases reluctantly, put aside their gene-splicing equipment and made arrangements to be in California for the conference. The conference turned out to be a major turning point in twentieth-century science, perhaps more so than most of those attending would have guessed.

The second Asilomar conference was held in February 1975. Perhaps the most important thing about the conference is that it represented the first time that all or nearly all scientists in a field had actually sat down to discuss the risks of a new area of research and development almost before that research and development had actually begun. Much of what was heard at Asilomar were disaster scenarios, and the stated goal of the meeting was to decide what could best be done to keep these scenarios from happening.

WORST-CASE SCENARIOS

The study of viral genes previously had been performed almost entirely by microbiologists, who had been trained in the techniques of viral containment; that is, they knew how to keep viruses in the laboratory where they belonged. They washed their hands carefully after working with viral organisms, they used special containment facilities so that the viruses could not escape from the experimental apparatus, and so forth.

Recombinant DNA techniques, however, allowed molecular biologists—scientists who study the molecules of which cells are made—to handle viral genes. The microbiologists argued that they were not properly trained. What if they forgot to wash their hands at a crucial moment or used improperly designed containment facilities or the wrong containment techniques? They might accidentally carry a recombinant bacterium out of the laboratory, either on their hands or (perhaps worse) in their gut. (Remember that E. coli normally lives in the human intestine.)

The recombinant bacterium might then spread to other individuals. If it contained viral genes it might be capable of causing viral diseases. Because E. coli is so "friendly" to human beings, it might be an unusually contagious disease, resulting in an unusually widespread and vicious epidemic. In a worst-case scenario, it might result in the total extinction of the human race.

Another scenario suggested that even the benevolent use of recombinant DNA techniques might have unexpected results, even if the experiment itself did not precisely go awry. The problem, it was suggested, is that our knowledge of the way in which genes and cells and even the human body itself behave is incomplete.

Suppose, for instance, that a well-meaning scientist decided that it would be useful if human beings could eat grass, like cows. Conceivably, he could create a recombinant E. coli bacterium that is capable of synthesizing an enzyme called cellulase, which breaks down cellulose fibers in grass into a digestible form. Then humans could eat grass just as cows do. (In fact, it is cellulase-producing bacteria in the intestines of cows that allow them to digest grass.)

Why would anyone do this? Well, perhaps it would be seen as a possible solution to famine. If food was unavailable, starving people could eat widely available grass until more traditional food became available. Many lives could be saved.

Unfortunately, a more likely result is that the cellulase-producing E. coli would kill human beings all by itself. We need undigested fiber in our intestines to prevent cancer and constipation; cellulase-producing bacteria would keep such fiber from ever reaching the lower intestines and the result would likely be disastrous.

Although nobody is likely to perform such an experiment (since the consequences are known), there are other experiments that might seem beneficial at first but would later turn out to have disastrous consequences after they are performed—when it might well be too late to reverse the damage that had already been done.

Yet another scenario suggested that genetic engineering was breaking down barriers that nature had put in place for good and solid reasons. By crossing the evolutionary barriers between a bacterial cell and, say, a human gene, scientists were tampering with hybrid combinations that were not meant to exist. Inevitably disaster of one sort or another would occur.

REBUTTALS TO
DISASTER SCENARIOS

Most scientists at Asilomar, however, objected to these scenarios. Recombinant E. coli bacteria, for instance, had been made so feeble by long years of residence in the laboratory (and by the recombinant DNA "surgery" itself) that they could never survive in the wild, that is, in the outside world. Even if they were capable of causing diseases, which was unlikely, they would die before they ever had the chance to do so, losing out in competition with nonengineered bacteria for such vital resources as food and living space.

Indeed, there were virtually no grounds for assuming that viral genes isolated in an E. coli bacterium would even be capable of causing disease. Viruses destroy cells when all of their genes work in concert to create new viruses. Isolated viral genes could perform no viral functions at all. In fact, viral genes are far less dangerous when inserted in a bacterium than they are when left in the virus.

Regarding the cellulase scenario, natural scientific caution would almost certainly nip such an outrageous plan in the bud before a "mad scientist" could unleash it on the world. Indeed, the existing procedures involved in approving drugs for human use would hardly allow such a destructive, if seemingly benevolent, treatment to slip into ordinary use.

As for the existence of supposed "evolutionary barriers" between bacteria and human cells, many biologists believed that no such barriers existed. Some scientists suggested that the *E. coli* in human intestines commonly mixes human genes with its own through naturally occurring processes. And dead plants and animals, lying decaying in the earth, commonly spread their genes into soil bacteria. So far, no super-disease-causing organisms seem to have been created by this process.

Nonetheless, the scientists at Asilomar began the process of drawing up guidelines for the research to be done with recombinant DNA techniques. Strict containment procedures were dictated for the experiments judged to be riskiest. The Recombinant DNA Advisory Committee (RAC) was founded under the auspices of the National Institutes of Health.

The most surprising result of Asilomar, however, was the sudden public awareness of recombinant DNA technology. What had only months before been an obscure research technique used by molecular biologists to study genes had now become widely publicized and controversial. Newspapers, catching wind of the conference and its potential for headlines, wrote about genetic engineering as though it were something out of a science fiction movie. And perhaps, to the general public, it was.

THE AFTERMATH
OF ASILOMAR

The reaction to Asilomar by nonscientists was rapid and intense. Special-interest groups were quickly formed to call for an end to the research. Worst of all, from the viewpoint of the scientists attending Asilomar, it was assumed by many members of the general public that if scientists were willing to admit that there were any dangers in recombinant DNA research—something that scientists in other fields had been notably reluctant to do in the past—then the danger must be even worse than they were admitting. Far from being an attempt to assess the risks of genetic engineering, Asilomar must be an attempt to cover it up.

But the opposition was indicative of a mutual distrust between scientists and the general public that had grown over the previous several decades, roughly since the development of the atomic bomb in 1945. More and more, nonscientists had come to see the scientific community as harboring terrible secrets that could threaten the very existence of the human race, and the scientists had come to see the general public as a suspicious and distrustful group that would like nothing better than to take away money from scientists involved in cutting-edge research. In this atmosphere of mutual suspicion and distrust, scientists and the public had grown farther and farther apart.

In all fairness, the public reaction to Asilomar was not all negative—and not all irrational. A citizens' committee formed in Cambridge, Massachusetts, in the late 1970s, for instance, voted to allow recombinant DNA research to continue in local university laboratories. Presented with the relevant facts, the nonscientists on the committee weighed the issues fairly and reasonably, coming to a sensible conclusion.

Asilomar, in retrospect, seems to have been a genuine attempt on the part of molecular biologists to assess the risks of their work. But the public overreaction to Asilomar so terrified many of the scientists who were there that if anything they became more secretive about their work in the wake of the conference.

Fortunately, the recombinant DNA techniques explored at Asilomar proved ultimately to be rather harmless. No vicious, disease-causing bacteria were created in subsequent experiments, and there were no cataclysmic consequences brought on by the crossing of evolutionary barriers. Of course, time may still reveal unexpected complications from this early genetic research, but so far there have been no unexpected results.

Although the RAC still oversees genetic engineering research and technology, the restrictions established during and after the second Asilomar conference have been greatly relaxed. Recombinant DNA research is now considered by most scientists to be much less dangerous than, say, traditional virus research.

You might wonder what all the fuss was about. If recombinant DNA techniques are merely a way of studying genes, what precisely is the problem?

The answer is that recombinant DNA techniques are much more than merely a way of studying genes. For one thing, they are an extremely powerful method of studying living cells and have taught scientists more about the nature of living organisms in the decade and a half that they have been used than had been learned in the centuries of research into living organisms that had preceded them.

But, perhaps even more importantly, recombinant DNA techniques opened the door to a genetic technology that could be used to revolutionize medicine. Once it became possible to splice new genes into bacteria, it became possible to manufacture substances with a tremendous battery of uses in medical treatment. For instance, the genes for human hormones, which are a type of protein molecule important in the metabolic functioning of the body, could be spliced into bacteria and produced in great quantity. Human insulin, which is desperately needed by persons suffering from diabetes, could be manufactured with the aid of genetically engineered *E. coli*. Human growth hormone could be manufactured for the treatment of dwarfism. All that needs to be done is to splice the appropriate gene into a bacterium, allow the bacterium to multiply, and siphon off the protein molecules thus produced. (Obviously, the process is a little more complicated than this makes it sound, but the difficulties are technical and have largely been solved.)

Recombinant DNA research also opens the door to a technology that had previously been thought almost unimaginable: the possibility of altering not only the genes of bacteria but the genes of human beings. This new technology offers the potential of curing diseases previously thought incurable, extending the human life span—even altering the nature of what it means to be human.

Part Three
SOCIETY

CHAPTER 7
READING
THE GENES

It is the year 2005. You are applying for a job with Megalopolitan Enterprises. An impeccably dressed executive sits across from you, studying your job application. He nods his head approvingly and finally smiles.

"Everything seems to be in order," he says finally. "But there's one small detail we'll need to take care of before we can welcome you to a new job here at Megalopolitan. If you'll excuse me for a moment . . ."

He turns to a computer perched on the edge of his desk, punching data into the keys. He stares at the screen for a moment, then frowns.

"I'm afraid we're not going to be able to hire you after all," he says. "According to this report from the company doctor who gave you your physical, you have a 35 percent chance of developing cancer before the age of fifty and a better than even chance of dying of a heart attack by sixty. Furthermore, you are unusually susceptible to small ailments and certain bone diseases. It would be very difficult to get you insured and it hardly seems worth putting you through our five-year executive training program. No, you'll just have to look for a job somewhere else. Have you considered waste management?"

As farfetched as this scenario may seem, it has already begun to come true. Although the idea of rejecting an applicant for a job because of a 35 percent chance of developing a disease may sound outlandish—who, after all, is in a position to make such a prediction? An astrologer?—it has nonetheless happened and may happen more and more often in the future. The problem, as Shakespeare might have said, lies not in our stars but in our genes.

GENETIC SCREENING

The technology of reading a person's genes to determine what diseases he or she may be susceptible to is called *genetic screening*. It is a technology that is still in its infancy, but it is already controversial. Genetic screening can be used to catch deadly diseases early in a person's life so that preventive measures can be taken before it is too late, but it also can be used to discriminate against individuals on the basis of what is in their chromosomes.

We saw in the last section how mistakes may occur in the copying of genes when cells divide. In many cases, these mistakes are harmless, producing new proteins that are functionally identical with the proteins the gene was intended to produce.

In other cases, the copying mistake kills the

organism of which the gene is part, because it can no longer function with the bad copy of the gene. This is particularly true if the bad gene was among the genes an organism inherits from one of its parents and therefore becomes part of all the cells in the organism's body.

Such deadly genes generally don't spread very far through a population of organisms because the organism that inherits one dies before it produces offspring to which it can pass the gene. Thus, bad genes tend to be weeded out of the population.

There are two cases, however, when this doesn't happen. The first is when the bad gene is not needed by the organism until the organism has grown older. Because most organisms reproduce earlier in life, the organism is not eliminated from the population until it has passed the gene to its offspring.

The second is when the bad gene is recessive. In most cases, recessive genes are not expressed unless they are received together with another, identical recessive gene. Thus, recessive bad genes can be passed down for generation after generation, spreading far and wide through a population, before they strike. Only when two individuals carrying the same recessive gene interbreed will the gene produce its deleterious effects. For this reason, many "bad" genes tend to be recessive. (This, in turn, is why closely related individuals should not produce offspring, since they probably will have several recessive genes in common.)

A surprisingly large number of devastating diseases are caused, not by viruses or bacteria, but by bad genes. Just some of the diseases known to be caused by one or more faulty genes include:

- *Phenylketonuria (PKU)*. An inherited disease that, if untreated, causes mental retardation. PKU affects the way the body metabolizes (processes) food. Children born with PKU are unable to metabolize part of a protein called phenylalanine, which then collects in the blood.
- *Thalassemia*. One of the most common inherited diseases of the blood, which primarily affects people of Italian and Greek descent. Thalassemia includes a number of different forms of anemia (red blood cell deficiency).
- *Tay-Sachs disease*. Caused by lack of a blood chemical that breaks down fatty deposits in brain and nerve cells. Tay-Sachs primarily affects people of Central and Eastern European Jewish descent, although members of any group may inherit the disease.
- *Neurofibromatosis (NF)*. Caused by small benign tumors (lumps) under the skin. NF may appear at any age, but especially during adolescence. Neurofibromatosis may either be inherited from a parent who has the disease or one in whom a mutation occurs. About 50 percent of NF cases occur in people with no family history of the disease.

Such conditions as heart disease and cancer, even if they are not strictly genetic conditions, may well have a genetic component; that is, a faulty gene may predispose a person toward these diseases.

Many of these diseases are probably caused by a single bad gene—a gene that either does not produce the protein that it is supposed to produce or does not produce enough of the protein or produces an imperfect version of the protein. Surprisingly small changes in the genes can produce devastating illnesses.

HUNTINGTON'S DISEASE: A GENETIC COIN TOSS

In light of this information, it's hard not to think of our chromosomes as time bombs ticking away inside our cells, waiting to spring some horrible illness on ourselves or our offspring. Consider the case of Huntington's disease.

Huntington's is a condition that strikes most victims between the ages of thirty-five and fifty, slowly destroying the nervous system until the sufferer is unable to speak or take care of himself or herself. It is a slow disease, taking ten to fifteen years to kill its victims. By all evidence, it is caused by a few defective genes and probably only a single defective gene.

The Huntington's gene is dominant, not recessive. If a parent passes the Huntington's gene to a child, then that child will eventually contract Huntington's—and will eventually die of it (assuming that they don't die of something else first). Thus, each child of a parent with Huntington's has a fifty-fifty chance of receiving the gene, assuming that the parent is heterozygous for Huntington's.

Possessing the Huntington's gene is effectively a death sentence. The gene works inevitably but inexorably to kill the individual in whose cells the gene resides. Someday there may be a cure for Huntington's, but for the present there is none.

Individuals with a parent who suffers from Huntington's know that they have a fifty-fifty chance of carrying the gene themselves. But the gene will not manifest itself until early middle age. Persons

carrying the gene must go through life wondering whether that life will be cut short by this devastating disease. Perhaps even worse, they know that if they possess the gene there is a fifty-fifty chance that they will pass that gene to each of their children. (The grandchildren of a Huntington's victim have a 25 percent chance of possessing the gene, given that their parent has a 50 percent chance.)

What if individuals had a way of learning whether they had the gene or not, before they develop the disease? Such knowledge would end the uncertainties that stretch on for decades and would help them make decisions about whether or not to have children. On the other hand, such knowledge could lead to even more dreadful uncertainty if they learned that they did have the gene.

If you had a fifty-fifty chance of carrying the Huntington's gene and were offered the opportunity to learn whether you actually had it or not, would you take it? Would you risk learning that you definitely had the gene in return for the chance of learning that you definitely did *not* have it? Is it better, in such circumstances, to go through life wondering . . . or to know?

In fact, this is the choice that is now available to children of Huntington's victims. There is a test that will, in most cases, determine whether an individual does or does not carry the Huntington's genes.

Woman with Huntington's disease. A new test that detects genetic markers for this disease has recently become available.

Many potential carriers have taken the test, but many more have refused to do so.

The test works like this: A chromosome contains many genes. When a parent passes these genes to an offspring, several genes tend to be passed together, because they are physically linked. (This isn't absolutely true; there is a phenomenon called crossing over that allows parts of two chromosomes in a pair to mix together in a hybrid chromosome that contains parts of both. But genes that lie close together on a chromosome do tend to be inherited together.) The exact location of the Huntington's gene among the human chromosomes is not known, though it is known that it is somewhere on the fourth chromosome. By analyzing the genes of several members of a family in which Huntington's is known to run, it is possible to find certain *markers* that are inherited together with the Huntington's gene in that family.

A marker is a stretch of DNA that lies near the Huntington's gene (or any other gene a scientist may be searching for) on the chromosome. The chromosome that may or may not carry the Huntington's gene can be sliced apart using restriction enzymes and mixed together with gene fragments known to carry the Huntington's marker. If the marker fragments pair off with some of the fragments being studied, bonding together according to the rules of base pairing, then the marker must be present on those fragments—therefore the Huntington's gene is almost certainly present too. Such a test can determine with a fair amount of certainty whether an individual's chromosomes carry the Huntington's gene, assuming that samples of DNA are available from enough other members of the family to make it possible to find suitable markers.

The Huntington's test became available in the mid-1980s. Before it became available, surveys were taken among those at risk of the disease to find out how many would want to take it. Roughly 70 percent of those polled indicated that they would. Only about 20 percent, however, actually took the test when it was first offered.

It's not hard to understand why those at risk would be reluctant to take the test. Uncertainty can be difficult, but certainty can be even worse. As long as potential victims don't know whether or not they carry the gene, they can always hope for the best. But there is a 50 percent chance that the test will take away that hope, leaving them with the far worse uncertainty about just when the disease will begin to take effect.

Medical personnel agree that whether or not to take the test is a personal decision—nobody should be forced to take the Huntington's test against his or her will. Even more importantly, it should be the decision of the person who takes the test as to whether anyone else should receive the information.

Why is this important? Well, place yourself back in the scenario with which we began this chapter. Suppose you are applying for a job and your prospective employer has access to your medical records. Would an employer want to take on a long-term employee at risk of developing a debilitating disease within only a few years?

Or suppose you were applying for health insurance. If the insurer knew that you were suffering from a condition that would require long-term, expensive care in the near future, would it be willing to offer you insurance? And if it did offer you insurance, would it offer a policy at a rate that you could afford? Yet, if you did not have insurance, could you afford to develop the disease that was steadily brewing in your genes?

And what of your relationships with other people? Would your friends look at you differently if they knew how you were going to die? Would they look at you as a victim instead of as just another human being? Would they treat you with unwanted pity? Or with unwanted scorn and fear?

Huntington's is an unusual case. Few diseases can be predicted with such accuracy. (Even with Huntington's, the predictions are not absolute. Some of those who have applied for the test have not been able to provide sufficient data from their relatives for the test to work. And in about 7 percent of cases, genetic crossover can misplace a marker and make the test inaccurate.) But even in the absence of absolute proof that individuals will develop a disease, there have been a number of cases in which individuals have been discriminated against because of supposedly dangerous genes.

SICKLE-CELL ANEMIA

Sickle-cell anemia is a case in point. It is a blood disease that is passed genetically from parent to child, mostly among blacks. It is caused by a faulty gene that prevents blood cells from forming correctly, thus preventing oxygen from being carried in the blood. It comes in two forms, depending on how many genes are inherited for the trait. An individual who is homozygous for sickle-cell anemia—that is, who inherits sickle-cell genes from both parents— will have the debilitating form of the disease and will probably die at a relatively young age. On the other hand, an individual who is heterozygous for sickle-cell anemia—that is, who inherits sickle-cell genes from only one parent—will have what is called sickle-cell trait.

A person with sickle-cell trait will have some improperly formed blood cells, but will have enough normal cells that oxygen will be properly carried in the blood. Such a person can lead a perfectly normal life, perhaps never realizing that he or she even carries the sickle-cell gene. Nonetheless, there is some evidence that individuals who carried the sickle-cell trait might be unusually susceptible to oxygen deprivation.

Accordingly, the Air Force Academy declared in the 1970s that it would no longer accept applicants for flight school who carried the sickle-cell trait. The reasoning behind this decision was that sickle-cell gene carriers might have difficulty in the rarefied air at high altitudes. The problem with the decision was that the evidence that showed that the sickle-cell trait predisposed carriers to high-altitude problems was not conclusive. And, because most carriers of the sickle-cell gene are black, it amounted to a kind of de facto racial discrimination.

The Air Force Academy was not the only organization to discriminate against job applicants who carried the sickle-cell gene; some airlines also followed suit. And, in some instances, the genetic screening for the gene was required only of black applicants—even though nonblacks occasionally display the trait as well.

Is it fair to discriminate against job applicants on the basis of the genes that they carry in their chromosomes? Surely if the genes have no relevance to the job, it isn't fair, no more so than discriminating against individuals because their genes have determined that they will be black or female. But if a prospective employer suspects that an applicant's genes will interfere with his or her ability to perform the job—is it fair then? Who decides what kind of genetic makeup is appropriate for a job?

"LIFE INSURANCE POLICIES WILL BE ESSENTIALLY ACCIDENT POLICIES"

And what of insurance? Does an insurance company have the right to perform a genetic screening of an individual before selling health insurance coverage and to set the price of that coverage, or even to determine whether or not an individual receives coverage at all, on the basis of that screening? Insurance companies argue that it would hardly be fair to make healthy applicants pay the costs of treatment for those who are genetically prone to debilitating disease. Consumer advocates, on the other hand, argue that this is the very purpose of insurance: to spread the cost of debilitating disease over a large number of relatively healthy individuals so that no one person is caught with catastrophically large medical costs.

The problem, of course, is that disease in the past was generally viewed as a random event. Whether you developed cancer or were stricken with a heart attack was largely a matter of chance, given that you ate a good diet and kept yourself in reasonably good shape. And given that disease was a matter of chance, insurance was a gamble: the insurance company was gambling that you would not get sick (and that they would make a profit on your premiums), and you were gambling that you would get sick (and would therefore get more than you paid for). But as more and more diseases turn out to have genetic components, illness seems less random and more predestined. In a world where illness can be predicted, is there any role for insurance at all?

"I can see twenty or thirty years from now," says Mark Rothstein, director of the Health Law Institute of the University of Houston, "that life insurance policies will be essentially accident policies, because everything else is foreseeable. The essence of insurance is you assess a risk against the unknown: if there's no unknown, the only unknown is whether you're going to get hit by a bus, right?"[1]

Rothstein may be exaggerating somewhat—some devastating illnesses are almost certainly nongenetic—but he has a point. Life insurance policies, of course, have long been based on medical diagnoses and such factors as the applicant's age and occupation. But life insurance is considered a luxury, something that is nice to have but isn't necessary to an individual's survival. What of health insurance, which helps people pay major medical costs that they might not otherwise be able to manage? If insurance ceases to exist, or if insurance companies become unwilling to support those whose genetic screenings are not up to par, how will society support the sick? How will victims of Huntington's or genetically caused cancer or heart attacks pay their medical costs?

The answer may be legislation that determines how far insurance companies are allowed to go in screening for genetic illness. Similar legislation has already been taken in several states to prevent insurance companies from discriminating against those infected with the virus that causes AIDS, a non-genetic disease that nonetheless can be medically predicted many years in advance.

There are already several dozen conditions for which genetic screening can be performed, and, in the future, there will probably be hundreds. (We'll have more to say about the future of genetic screening in the next chapter.) Already doctors can use genetic analysis to determine who is at greater than average risk of having a heart attack or developing certain forms of cancer. As the number of diseases that can be screened in advance grows, the problem of how to deal responsibly with that information grows as well. In the next chapter, we'll look at a government-sponsored project that will greatly increase our knowledge of human chromosomes—and that may well increase the problems associated with that knowledge.

CHAPTER 8
CATALOGING
THE GENES

It is the year 2025. The director of a super-secret new government security agency sits behind his desk, studying the screen of his computer. Names and numbers flash by as he knits his brow in consternation. An assistant sits by his side, watching him intently.

"It doesn't look good," he says finally. "If these figures are correct, we only have another twenty years before the Neo-Federalist party will be voted out of office. There will be a major shift among voters to the Crypto-Whig party."

"But that's terrible!" says the assistant. "The Crypto-Whigs believe all the wrong things—and a Crypto-Whig president would surely abolish our super-secret agency, assuming he finds out about it!"

"I know," replies the director, nodding his head. "That's why we must develop an emergency plan. According to the data, the majority of children born after this year will have a genetic predisposition to vote for Crypto-Whigs, so we must do something before it is too late."

"It shouldn't be hard to do a little genetic tampering," suggests the assistant. "We'll see that the current president passes proper legislation to be sure that parents with Crypto-Whig genes are not allowed to marry others with the same gene. After all, the Crypto-Whig gene is recessive. Do you think the president will go along with that?"

"Oh, yes," says the director. "I know a few things about *his* genes too!"

This scenario seems even more outlandish than the one at the beginning of the previous chapter, and perhaps it is. But scenarios very much like it have been suggested as a possible result of genetic research. Nonetheless, there is a government project even now in the beginning stages that, if successful, will tell us almost everything there is to know about our genes, whether we want to know it or not. Within a few short decades it could revolutionize the way medicine is performed, even put an end to most genetic diseases (a possibility to be further explored in the next chapter). But it is controversial for a number of reasons, as we will see.

MAPPING THE GENES

The sum total of all the genes in an organism is referred to as that organism's *genome*. Within the genome are all the "recipes" for all the proteins that make that organism what it is. Dogs carry the dog genome in every one of their cells, cats carry the cat genome, and humans carry the human genome. The contents of those genes may vary slightly from individual to individual, but only slightly. Differences in genes between members of various species are somewhat greater, but not as great as you might guess. The difference between a human being and a cat is in only a small percent of their genes. The genetic difference between a human being and a chimpanzee, our closest evolutionary relative, is only about one percent.

Looked at as a repository of information, the human genome may be the most important "book" ever written—to humans, anyway. If we could read that book in its entirety—and if we understood what we were reading, which is not quite the same thing—we would know almost everything there is to know about ourselves. Or would we?

In recent years, some biologists have argued that the book of the human genome is too important to leave unread any longer. Granted, we already know a great deal about the human genome, as we saw in the last chapter. But there is far more that we don't know. It is high time, these biologists suggest, that we began mapping the human genome.

Reading genes is a time-consuming and tedious task. The nucleotides are too small to examine under a microscope; scientists must engage in clever subterfuge to read the contents of the chromosomes. But it can be done.

Mapping the genome actually refers to two different tasks. The first way of achieving a genome map is to determine which genes lie on which chromosomes at which position. There are organisms, such as the E. coli bacterium, that have had their genomes mapped in their entirety in this manner.

(This is why *E. coli* is so popular in recombinant DNA research: it is the most fully understood organism on earth.)

Thomas Hunt Morgan mapped the genes of the fruit fly early in this century. The method that he used involved the phenomenon of "crossing over" in genes.

We saw earlier that genes on the same chromosome tend to be inherited together, because they are physically linked. If your parents had Genes A and B on one chromosome and Genes C and D for the same traits on another chromosome, it would seem likely that you would receive Genes A and B together or C and D together but not B and C together, because those two traits are not on the same chromosome. Yet in practice it doesn't work this way. The two chromosomes can "cross over," that is, exchange large sections of nucleotides, so that Genes B and C could end up on the same chromosome and be inherited together.

The closer genes are to one another on the chromosome, the greater the chance that they will be inherited together. Thus, if Genes A and B are directly next to one another on a chromosome, you probably will get them together. If they are at opposite ends of the chromosome, they may be separated by crossover.

Morgan kept careful records of how traits were

Gene sequencing techniques have enabled scientists to determine that the genetic difference between a human being and a chimpanzee is only about one percent.

inherited from one generation of fruit flies to the next. Using statistical analysis, he was able to determine which traits were inherited together no more often than random chance would dictate (and which therefore must be in completely different chromosome pairs), which were inherited together a little more often than chance would dictate (and therefore must be at opposite ends of a chromosome), and which were inherited together almost invariably (and therefore must be very close together on a chromosome). In this way, he was able to put together a rough map of where these genes fell on the chromosome. Today, similar but more sophisticated methods of genetic analysis are used to map the positions of genes. Still, out of an estimated 100,000 genes in the human genome, fewer than 5,000 have been mapped to date.

The second thing that we mean when we speak of mapping the genome is determining the precise sequence of bases on every one of the chromosomes. This is a far more formidable task and has never been performed on a higher organism. The human genome consists of approximately three billion such bases (or, more accurately, pairs of bases), a large number by the standards of anyone except a federal budget director.

THE HUMAN GENOME PROJECT

The Human Genome Project, an initiative of the federal government, will attempt to perform the first stage of mapping—a detailed plan showing where every gene is on every chromosome—over a five-year period in the early 1990s. Over the next ten years the directors of the project hope to complete the second stage, a precise map of the sequence of three billion nucleotide pairs that comprise the human genome.

The project was officially initiated in January 1989, although the actual gene sequencing had not yet begun at the time this book was written in late 1989. It has been compared to the Apollo moon-landing program of the 1960s and the Manhattan Project, which built the first atomic bomb during World War II. It is a massive, and expensive, endeavor.

Surprisingly, it is quite controversial among biologists themselves, the very people who would seem to benefit the most from such information. Because of the expense of the project, estimated at $3 billion (a dollar per nucleotide?) over a fifteen-year period, many biologists fear that it will be harder to find funding for their own work. In the long run, biologists may benefit from the information, but in the short run biology in general may suffer. And some biologists wonder if the information is worth the cost.

The project has many supporters. Nobel Prize–winning biologist Walter Gilbert compares the sequencing of the genome to the medieval search for the Holy Grail. George Cahill of the Howard Hughes Medical Institute gushes: "It's going to tell us everything. Evolution, disease, everything will be based on what's in the magnificent tape called DNA.[2]"

Well, perhaps. But sequencing the genome will be just the beginning of science's effort to understand the genetic basis of humankind. Knowing what nucleotide or what gene lies where on the chromosome is not the same as knowing what those nucleotides and genes actually do. Many human

traits probably result from the coordinated action of several genes, something that will not necessarily be apparent from looking at the genes.

On the other hand, once the actual sequence of nucleotides is known, we probably will find many surprising things in that sequence. More tightly focused studies tend to find only those things that they are looking for; this sort of basic research into genetics could lead to unexpected discoveries.

One thing that scientists expect to find in the genome is junk. That's right: junk. It's been estimated that more than 90 percent of the nucleotide sequences in the chromosomes don't code for anything at all. They just take up space. Why should this be? One guess is that it's nature's way of providing for our evolutionary development. When mutations occur and precipitate sudden evolutionary changes in a species—"sudden" in this context meaning over a period of perhaps tens of thousands of years—changes may be the result of certain previously unused sections of the genome being abruptly turned on, or previously used sections being turned off. Some of this "junk DNA" may be the remains of functional gene sequences used by our ancestors that human beings don't use any more. And some of it may be gene sequences that our

James D. Watson, one of the discoverers of the structure of DNA. Watson was recently chosen to head the Human Genome Project. The goal of this project is to map the entire genetic makeup of humans.

distant descendants may someday use. This, in fact, may explain why the genetic differences between humans and other species are so small. The same genes are in the chromosomes, but different ones are being used.

It's also possible that some of this junk may turn out not to be junk after all. There is still much that is not understood about the way in which our genes work. For instance, how do certain cells know that they are supposed to be skin cells while certain other cells know that they are supposed to be lung cells and still other cells know that they are to be brain cells—when all of these cells contain exactly the same genes? Much has been theorized about this cellular differentiation and much is known about it. But there is much more to be known. Will these and other secrets be revealed by the Human Genome Project? Quite possibly they will be.

CAVEATS

Other people, scientists and concerned citizens, worry that we may be learning too much about the genome too soon. Given the sorts of worries about genetic screenings that we voiced in the last chapter, do we really need to know still more about how our genes work—and how they can fail to work? If the project is successful and the human genome is eventually understood in total, we will then know the genetic basis behind every inherited disease. More than that, we may well learn that there are in fact genes that predispose one person to be happy, another to be sad; one person to become a doctor, another to become a truck driver; one person to vote Democrat, another to vote Republican.

Of course, many of these things are probably not determined by genes at all: they are determined by the environment in which an individual grows up. But if by some chance it turns out that these things are in some way affected by genetic makeup, however subtly, do we really want this information in the wrong hands? Will some future dictator take control of our genes to secure his power, killing those who carry genes he disapproves of (or simply preventing the bearers of those genes from having children) and encouraging the proliferation of "desirable" genes?

This may be outlandish, but certain other possibilities hit closer to home. Some researchers now believe that mental conditions such as schizophrenia are inherited through the genes. Should schizophrenics not be allowed to have children because they may pass this gene on to another generation? Should fetuses identified as bearing the gene be aborted?

In time, a complete understanding of the genome could lead to the existence of genome data banks, where genetic information will be kept on all citizens. Insurance companies, government agencies, and anyone else with access to these banks could learn everything there is to know genetically about everyone: what diseases they are prone to, what mental conditions they may suffer from, even what sort of disposition they might have. The possibilities for abusing this information are immense.

But possibilities are not necessarily probabilities. Just because such data banks could exist doesn't necessarily mean that they will exist, even given perfect information about the human genome. New laws could restrict the use of genetic information, even banning the existence of such genetic data banks outright.

Knowledge is power and power can be abused. But without knowledge there can be no progress. The knowledge gained by the Human Genome Project, expensive as it will be, may lead to tremendous technological leaps.

Perhaps the greatest paradox of current genetic technology is that our ability to read problems in the genes has greatly outstripped our ability to solve those problems. We can diagnose diseases, but we cannot cure them.

This makes sense. You can't cure a disease that you don't understand, except by great good fortune. Once the causes of a disease are grasped, it takes time to find the cure—assuming a cure exists. And genetic diseases are particularly difficult to treat, because their causes are written in the book of genes itself.

But that is changing. As our knowledge of human genetics increases, we are coming closer to a day when we might be able to treat genetic illness using techniques that have come to be called *genetic surgery*. Once we have mastered these techniques, we will be able to offer hope to those who suffer from genetic conditions such as Huntington's: not only will we diagnose the faulty gene, but we will replace it with a gene that works.

Yet even this hopeful future has a shadow over it. If we can tamper with the genes in good ways, then we can tamper with them in bad ways as well. There are those who argue that this sort of human genetic engineering is morally wrong and should never be performed.

CHAPTER 9

REWRITING
THE GENES

It is the year 2035. The young couple sit side by side in the doctor's office, waiting for the results of the genetic testing on their unborn child. The doctor sits down opposite them and smiles.

"Congratulations, Mr. and Mrs. Smith!" announces the doctor. "It's a girl!"

The couple look disturbed. "Oh, but we were so much hoping for a boy!"

"Well," the doctor replies, "that can be easily changed. Just a little chromosome fiddling and your daughter will be a son."

"Perfect," the husband says. "I'm looking forward to playing football with him on our front lawn!"

"Ah," begins the doctor, "I'm afraid our analysis shows that she—I mean, he—will be more predisposed to dancing and music than to playing football."

"Can't you do something about that?" the husband asks. "I don't want a son who dresses up in a tutu and dances in a ballet!"

"Or plays loud music while I'm trying to sleep!" adds the wife.

"I suppose we can fix that, too," says the doctor. "After all, we'll be doing a routine chromosome fix to be sure that your child doesn't inherit any recessive traits that you may be carrying."

"And I hope that you make sure that he's an obedient child," the wife demands. "I don't want a son who talks back and doesn't listen to his mother!"

"There is a certain streak of rebelliousness in his genes," the doctor tells them. "But I'm sure we can take care of that, too. Never let it be said that a child I delivered was anything less than perfect."

GENETIC SURGERY

The first attempt at genetic surgery has already been made. It took place in 1979. Dr. Martin Cline of the University of California at Los Angeles took cells from the bone marrow of two young women, one in Italy and the other in Israel, both suffering from a disease called beta thalassemia. Like sickle-cell anemia, beta thalassemia is caused by a defect in the gene that codes for hemoglobin, the molecule in red blood cells that permits them to transport oxygen from the lungs to the body. The disease is debilitating and painful, and victims usually die by the age of twenty.

Cline incubated the bone marrow cells in a solution containing hemoglobin genes produced using recombinant DNA techniques. In theory, the genes should have entered the bone marrow cells and begun producing functional hemoglobin molecules. Cline then reinjected the treated solution into the young women.

He had hoped that the newly introduced hemo-globin genes would continue producing hemoglobin in the women's bodies and cure, or at least alleviate, their condition. Unfortunately, he was unsuccess-ful. The "surgery" did not work.

To make matters worse, such surgery was forbid-den in the United States by the NIH guidelines that had been drafted at Asilomar. Cline had not secured permission to perform the surgery. Although the experimental procedure had not taken place in the United States, he was accused upon his return of ignoring federal regulations. In the furor that fol-lowed, he resigned his job and was later disciplined by the NIH.

In the decade since, interest in genetic surgery among scientists and doctors has increased, but progress has been cautious. The idea behind genetic surgery is simple. If many diseases are caused by a faulty gene, then they can be cured by the introduc-tion of nonfaulty copies of the gene into the body. The major problems, obviously, are finding a way to get the new genes into the body, keeping them in the body once they are there, and coaxing them into expressing themselves—that is, manufacturing proteins—while they are there. So far, tentative so-lutions to all of these problems have been found, but a complete working method of performing genetic surgery has not.

Initially, it was assumed that the bone marrow was the most obvious place to put the new genes, as Cline demonstrated in his unsuccessful experi-ment. It is relatively simple to remove bone marrow from the body and to replace it.

Getting the new genes into the bone marrow cells while they are out of the body is a little trickier. The most ingenious method yet proposed is to use a retrovirus, nature's own genetic engineer, to do the job. A recombinantly engineered retrovirus, containing both viral genes and the genes to be inserted into the bone marrow, would be used to "infect" the marrow. As it is wont to do, the retrovirus would insert the genes into the chromosomes of the bone marrow cell, thus accomplishing the genetic surgery on the most microscopic of levels.

But repeated attempts to infect bone marrow cells with a recombinant retrovirus and force the genes to produce the wanted proteins have failed in the laboratory and would almost certainly fail in the operating room. Scientists have begun to wonder if there isn't a better way.

One method now being pioneered by the NIH is the development of artificial organs that can be implanted in the human body. Such organs would contain cells with the modified genes and would release the needed proteins into the body much like real organs. Experimental organs have already been made using the fiber laminate Gore-Tex, commonly used in the manufacture of thermal skiwear. The NIH hopes to use these organs in the treatment of AIDS, to release a protein called CD4 that may prevent the AIDS virus from infecting cells.

Other biologists have been studying human epithelial cells (the cells that line the lungs and blood vessels) as candidates for genetic surgery. Experiments have shown that these cells are readily

AIDS-infected T4 lymphocytes.
The virus can be seen budding
from the membranes of the lymphocytes.

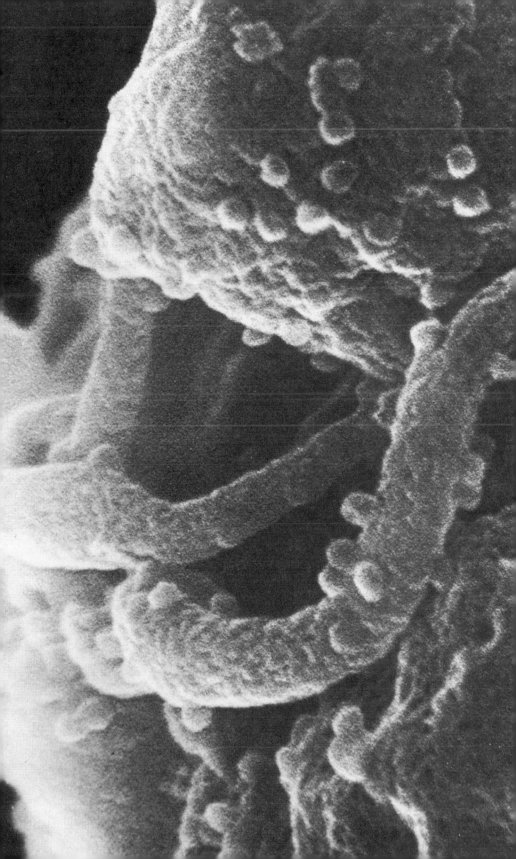

infected by retroviruses carrying recombinantly engineered genes. And, since they normally interact closely with the circulatory system, epithelial cells could be used to spread needed proteins throughout the body.

A PROMISING TECHNIQUE

In the spring of 1989, an experiment took place that may eventually be looked on as the true beginning of genetic surgery, after the abortive start a decade earlier by Dr. Cline. Three scientists at NIH designed an experiment in which cancer-fighting cells are removed from the bodies of patients suffering from terminal melanoma and are injected with an artificially created virus; then the cells are reinjected into the patients. Eventually, the scientists hope to use this technique to place powerful anticancer proteins into the patients' body. In this experiment, however, the protein produced by the virus had no therapeutic value; it was merely a "marker" protein that would demonstrate whether the technique is really workable. The actual treatment will be tried only if the experiment is a success.

Several months after the experiment was performed, the scientists announced that the marker genes had circulated through the bodies of the patients for at least nineteen days and apparently were secreting their proteins. The experiment, then, was a success. Furthermore, the scientists who performed it have already succeeded in creating a similar cell that will secrete a cancer-fighting compound, though it has not yet been injected into a patient.

This technique obviously has promise beyond

fighting cancer. If cells containing recombinant genes can be injected into the body and survive there for weeks at a time, then such cells can be used to deliver treatment for any number of genetic diseases. Genetic surgery may offer a cure for any disease that results from one or a few defective genes. But it may be some time before the technique is perfected. Unseen obstacles may still lie ahead.

ETHICAL DILEMMAS

Before the initial experiment was performed, however, the Recombinant DNA Advisory Committee (RAC) held a public meeting at which a group of activists and concerned citizens met with scientists and voiced their feelings about the directions that this research might take in the future.

The most outspoken person at the meeting was Jeremy Rifkin, who has been a critic of genetic engineering since the 1970s. With him were a number of advocates for the disabled, many of them suffering from genetic diseases of precisely the sort that genetic therapy is intended to cure. Their fear is that they will not be given a voice in the development of their own treatment, and that such treatment, when developed, will be forced on them by insurance companies who will otherwise refuse to pay the cost of their care, whether or not they wish to take the treatment voluntarily. "Believe it or not," said one attendee, "we are not all in a rush to be cured or prevented."[3]

The major point made by those attending was that the RAC, which consists of seventeen scientists and eight laypersons, was not sufficient to make decisions about experiments in genetic therapy.

Rifkin called for the establishment of an advisory group that he has named the Human Eugenics Advisory Committee, which would consist of civil liberties experts and advocates for disabled workers and consumers.

The ultimate fear of those opposed to genetic surgery is that it will eventually become mandatory. People with the "wrong" genes will be forced to have the "right" ones.

But who will decide what the difference is between a wrong gene and a right one? Clearly genes that cause pain, death, and suffering are "wrong," but such clear-cut cases can lead to more questionable circumstances where genetic surgery will be performed with less and less provocation. Is your child rebellious? Change his genes. Is someone voicing the wrong political opinion? Change her genes.

Once we can change the genes of adults, why not change the genes of their children—before they are born? By altering the *germ cells*, the cells that are passed on at conception, a new type of child can be created, one whose genes are permanently altered and who will pass those alterations on to his or her children as well. Such germ cell surgery is generally agreed to be morally wrong, because once done it cannot be undone. Current schemes for genetic surgery are not long-lasting; at their best they will persist for the lifetime of the patient. But germ cell surgery is forever.

Gene surgery is one of the most powerful techniques on the medical horizon and it must be approached warily. It will cure diseases that can be cured in no other manner, but it can also be used to alter human beings in ways that we might ultimately regret. It is necessary that we approach this technology cautiously but with hope, with our eyes open both to the possibilities and to the perils. As the turn of the millennium approaches, society must be open to technological advances, but it must not be blind to ways in which those advances can be abused.

EPILOGUE

BEYOND
GENE TECHNOLOGY

The late philosopher C. P. Snow once observed that there were two "cultures" in modern society, a culture of scientists and a culture of nonscientists. Although the two cultures live side by side, they have relatively little interaction. Scientists go their own way, doing what it is that scientists do, and nonscientists go their own way, too.

According to Snow, the two cultures had gone their own way because they had lost the ability to communicate. Nonscientists long ago had ceased to understand what the scientists were talking about (and, indeed, had decided that they were not capable of understanding). Scientists, on the other hand, had little interest in the more intellectual aspects of the culture of the nonscientists.

This is still true. But the nonscientists, for their part, have come to recognize that what scientists do has a direct effect on their lives. Nuclear weapons, communications satellites, recombinant DNA experiments—the nonscientist may not understand what makes these things tick, but he or she knows full well that they have changed the world. And not always for the better.

Scientists, in turn, have come to realize that their livelihood is at least partly in the hands of the nonscientists. Science in the twentieth century has become an expensive endeavor, and it is the politicians and voters who decide, in large part, where the money comes from to support science. They can also decide what kind of science gets supported. And they can pass laws against forms of scientific activity that they believe to be dangerous.

Thus, the two cultures need one another. Scientists and engineers bestow new and useful technologies on the nonscientists, and the nonscientists supply money and the sanction of society on the actions of the scientists.

What a pity, then, that these two cultures have come increasingly to fear and distrust one another. Scientists, most of whom genuinely believe that their activities will make the world a better place, fear that a misguided, largely nonscientific public may put an end to their most promising lines of research, either through legislation or withdrawal of funds. And the nonscientific public, understanding that scientists make mistakes and can sometimes convince themselves that the risks of their experimentation are less than is actually the case, fears that uncontrolled technological and scientific growth may reduce their own quality of life.

In short, there is a distinct lack of trust between the two cultures. Scientists distrust the nonscientific public, and nonscientists distrust the scientific establishment.

The only cures for distrust are knowledge and honesty. You, the reader of this book, will someday make a choice as to which of these cultures you will become part of; perhaps you have already made that choice. If you become a scientist, bear in mind that you are obligated to keep your work as open and accessible to the public as possible. If you do not become a scientist but are concerned about the impact that science and technology have on your world, you have an obligation to understand, at least in general terms, what it is that scientists are actually doing and what kind of risks are involved.

You have incurred these obligations as a member of a democratic society, where the future is often determined by majority vote and by the actions of concerned citizens. As a voter and a citizen, you can decide whether technologies such as those discussed in this book produce benefits commensurate with the risks involved. You can make those decisions at the ballot box or, better still, as a member of a citizens' committee. But in order to make those decisions, you must first learn about the benefits and risks of the technology in question.

This book has attempted to give you some of the information you need in order to make decisions concerning a particular scientific issue: gene technology. There are more books on this subject listed in the bibliography and you are encouraged to read some of these as well.

The more knowledge you have on a subject such as gene technology, the better able you will be to make the sort of decisions that are required of you as a citizen—and the better the future that will come about as a direct result of those decisions.

NOTES

1. "Predisposition and Prejudice." *Science News*. 21 January 1989, 42.
2. "The Gene Hunt." *Time*. 20 March 1989, 63.
3. "Ethical Questions Haunt New Genetic Technologies." *Science*. 3 March 1989, 1134.

GLOSSARY

Amino acids. The chemical "building blocks" that are linked together to form proteins. All proteins are made from the same set of twenty different amino acids.

Amniocentesis. A medical procedure allowing doctors to examine the amniotic fluid that surrounds the unborn baby in the mother's womb.

Anticodon. The sequence of three bases on the transfer RNA molecule that recognizes a complementary sequence of three bases on the messenger RNA.

Bacteriophage. A virus that infects bacteria. It lives and multiplies inside the bacterium.

Bacterium. A microorganism, such as *E. coli*, with a cell wall and a chromosome not enclosed within a nucleus.

Bases. The set of chemical substances present in DNA and RNA: adenine, guanine, thymine, cytosine, and uracil. Their sequence in DNA contains the genetic information.

Cell. A microscopic structure of plant or animal life, consisting of living matter within a membrane.

Chromosomes. Threadlike structures in the cells. Chromosomes carry hereditary material in the form of genes.

Cleaving. A term applied to the cutting of DNA strands at specific sites by means of restriction enzymes. Also called *cleavage.*

Clone. One of a group of genetically identical cells all descended from a single common parent cell.

Codon. The sequence of three bases on DNA or RNA that codes for a particular amino acid.

Complementary bases. The exact pairing of bases that bind strands of nucleic acid together. In DNA, adenine always pairs with thymine, and guanine always pairs with cytosine; in RNA, adenine always pairs with uracil.

DNA. The chemical compound deoxyribonucleic acid, which contains the hereditary information in a cell.

DNA ligase. An enzyme that helps in joining the two DNA strands that make up the double helix. Also aids in repairing damaged DNA.

DNA polymerase. One of the enzymes involved in DNA replication. It helps position the proper nucleotides onto the template and supplies the energy to join them together to form a chain.

Double helix. The 3-D structure of the DNA molecule. The structural model of DNA, first conceived by Francis Crick and James Watson, consists of two long strands of DNA twisted about each other.

E. coli. A common type of bacteria found in the human intestines. Many strains of the *E. coli* bacteria are used in gene splicing.

Enzymes. Proteins that act to speed up the chemical reactions found in all biological systems.

Eukaryotes. A general name for organisms whose cells contain a nucleus and more than one chromosome.

Fetus. An unborn animal in the intermediate and late stages of formation. In humans, the fetal stage lasts from the ninth week until birth.

Gene mapping. Locating the positions of the genes on the chromosomes of a particular organism.

Genes. Molecules of DNA (or, in certain viruses, RNA) that are carried on the chromosomes. Each gene carries the code for synthesis of a specific protein.

Genetic code. The relationship linking the sequence of bases in DNA or RNA to the sequence of amino acids in proteins.

Genome. The section of DNA that carries the complete set of genetic instructions for an organism.

Genotype and phenotype. Terms used to distinguish between the genetic constitution of an organism (genotype) and the observable constitution (phenotype).

Germ cell. An egg or sperm cell.

Heterozygous. Carrying an unmatched gene for any particular autosomal hereditary trait (except for X-linked traits).

Homozygous. Carrying genes for any particular hereditary trait on each of two chromosomes.

Hybrid. Offspring of genetically diverse parents.

In vitro. The term literally means "in glass." In vitro lab experiments are distinguished from those performed directly on animals or humans (in vivo).

Karyotype. The organized chart of the chromosomes of a cell. A karyotype is made for the purpose of counting and examining chromosomes.

Messenger RNA (mRNA). The intermediate RNA molecule that is synthesized in the cell nucleus according to instructions encoded in the DNA. It then moves out into the body of the cell, carrying its "message" to the ribosomes, where the proteins are made.

Microorganisms. General term for microscopic plant or animal life.

Mitochondria. Tiny bodies found in all cells. They contain enzymes that aid in the release of energy from food. Frequently called the "powerhouses" of cells.

Mitosis. The process by which cells usually divide and multiply.

Molecular biology. The study of the molecular structure and chemical reactions of living cells.

Molecule. The smallest subunit of a compound, consisting of two or more atoms.

Monoclonal antibodies. Genetically engineered antibodies derived from hybrid cancer and antibody-producing cells that are cloned and cultured to produce pure, specific antibodies.

Mutation. A change in the genes caused by alteration in the structure of its DNA.

—115

Nucleotide. A chemical compound that consists of a base, a sugar, and one or more phosphate groups. The basic structural unit of DNA and RNA.

Organism. Any form of life having one or more cells, including bacteria, plants, and humans.

Phage. See *Bacteriophage.*

Phenotype. See *Genotype and phenotype.*

Plasmids. Small, circular DNA molecules present in bacteria that are accessories to a bacteria's chromosomes. They reproduce independently and enable bacteria to transfer genetic material among themselves.

Prokaryotes. Those organisms whose cells have no nuclear membrane and only one chromosome.

Proteins. One of the most important groups of biological molecules. All enzymes are proteins, but not all proteins are enzymes. All proteins are constructed from combinations of the same set of twenty amino acids.

Recombinant DNA. The creation of a new DNA molecule by the process of cleaving and rejoining different DNA strands.

Replication. The process whereby DNA reproduces itself.

Restriction enzyme. An enzyme that recognizes a specific base sequence in DNA and cuts, or cleaves, the DNA chain at a specific site.

Retrovirus. A virus whose genetic material is RNA. A retrovirus enters the lost cell, where the viral RNA is transcribed into DNA.

Ribosomal RNA (rRNA). The form of RNA that is the major component of ribosomes.

Ribosome. A complex structure found in cells that acts as the site for protein synthesis. It is made up of proteins and ribosomal RNA.

RNA. Ribonucleic acid (RNA) is a chemical relative of DNA. It is usually a single-stranded molecule that differs from DNA in using the sugar ribose in its nucleotide backbone and in substituting the base uracil for thymine.

Sex chromosomes. The chromosomes that determine gender. In humans, females have two X chromosomes (XX). Males have an X and a Y chromosome (XY).

Synthesis. The making of a complex chemical substance by combining simpler compounds or elements.

Transcription. The process by which the genetic information in DNA is copied to form messenger RNA (mRNA) molecules.

Transfer RNA (tRNA). A form of RNA that is coded to collect the amino acids needed for protein synthesis and "transfer" them to their proper position on messenger RNA at the ribosomes. There is at least one transfer RNA molecule for each kind of amino acid.

Transformation. A process of introducing foreign DNA, such as plasmids, into a bacterial cell.

Translation. The process by means of which the genetic message carried by messenger RNA directs the synthesis of a protein molecule on a ribosome.

Vector. A vehicle for moving DNA from one cell to another, such as a plasmid into which foreign DNA can easily be inserted and which will be efficiently taken up by the host cell.

Virus. A disease-causing agent that consists of a core of DNA or RNA enclosed in a protective coat. Viruses reproduce only in living cells.

SOURCES USED

Chakrabarty, Ananda, ed. *Genetic Engineering*. Boca Raton, Fla.: CRC Press, 1978.

Emery, Alan E. *An Introduction to Recombinant DNA*. New York: Wiley, 1984.

Friedman, Theodore. *Gene Therapy: Fact and Fiction in Biology's New Approach to Disease*. Cold Spring Harbor, N.Y.: Cold Spring Harbor Laboratory, 1983.

Goodfield, June. *Playing God: Genetic Engineering and the Manipulation of Life*. New York: Random House, 1977.

Karp, Laurence E. *Genetic Engineering, Threat or Promise?* Chicago: Nelson-Hall, 1976.

Kevles, Daniel J. *In the Name of Eugenics: Genetics and the Uses of Human Heredity*. New York: Knopf, 1985.

Lappe, Marc. *Broken Code: The Exploitation of DNA*. San Francisco: Sierra Club Books, 1984.

Office of Technology Assessment. *Genetic Technology: A New Frontier*. Boulder, Co.: Westview Press, 1982.

Santos, Miguel A. *Genetics and Man's Future: Legal, Social and Moral Implications of Genetic Engineering.* Springfield, Ill.: CC Thomas, 1981.

Sasson, Albert. *Biotechnologies: Challenges & Promises.* Lanham, Md.: UNESCO, 1984.

Sylvester, Edward J. *The Gene Age: Genetic Engineering and the Next Industrial Revolution.* New York: Scribner, 1987.

Yoxen, Edward. *The Gene Business: Who Should Control Biotechnology?* New York: Oxford University Press, 1986.

FOR FURTHER READING

Engdahl, Sylvia Louise. *Tool for Tomorrow: New Knowledge About Genes.* New York: Atheneum, 1979.

Lampton, Chris. *DNA and the Creation of New Life.* New York: Arco, 1983.

Oleksy, Walter. *Miracles of Genetics.* Chicago: Childrens Press, 1986.

Silverstein, Alvin. *Futurelife, the Biotechnology Revolution.* Englewood Cliffs, N.J.: Prentice-Hall, 1982.

Silverstein, Alvin, and Virginia Silverstein. *The Genetics Explosion.* New York: Four Winds Press, 1980.

Stwertka, Eve, and Albert Stwertka. *Genetic Engineering,* rev. ed. New York: Franklin Watts, 1989.

INDEX

ABOUT
THE AUTHOR

Christopher Lampton has written over thirty books for young people on topics ranging from anthropology to computers. His recent books for Franklin Watts are *New Theories on the Dinosaurs, New Theories on the Origins of the Human Race,* and *Predicting Nuclear and Other Technological Disasters.* Mr. Lampton has also written four science fiction novels. He makes his home in Silver Spring, Maryland.